FEEL-GOOD
FALL BAKING

105 RECIPES THE WHOLE FAMILY WILL LOVE

CENTENNIAL KITCHEN®

CENTENNIAL BOOKS

FEEL-GOOD
FALL BAKING

105 RECIPES THE WHOLE FAMILY WILL LOVE

Pear Cobbler,
p. 127

Contents

Sweet Potato
Cupcakes With
Chocolate
Frosting, p. 42

Taste of the Season

If summer is all about grilling, fall is when we love to get back to baking. And with the grocery stores and farmers markets full of apples, pears, pumpkins, sweet potatoes, cranberries, pecans and walnuts that are practically *begging* to be made into pies, crisps, cobblers, cakes and quick breads, we can't wait to get back into the kitchen.

And there is no shortage of delicious recipes to put these fall flavors to work. Whether you're searching for something brand new or just want an update of a classic, there's something here for everyone, from beginner bakers to seasoned pros. Have you always been more of a pie eater than a pie maker? This cookbook will change that! Never worked with yeast before? Our easy bread recipes will transform you into a confident bread and focaccia chef.

Baking is also a great way to keep kids busy and make some memories—and what child wouldn't willingly volunteer to lick the bowl and spatula? And is there any better way to boost everyone's spirits than by pulling an old-fashioned Pumpkin Pie (p. 20), a Caramel Cheesecake (p. 34), Coconut Pecan Cookies (p. 82), or a fresh-baked Apple Crisp With Oatmeal Cookie Crust (p. 128) from the oven? We hope these delicious recipes bring your family lots of enjoyment and time together!

Pies & Tarts

SPOTLIGHT CLASSIC FALL INGREDIENTS AND FLAVORS—APPLES, PEARS, PUMPKIN SPICE, CARAMEL— WITH THESE DELICIOUS RECIPES THAT ARE EASY TO WHIP UP FOR FAMILY MEALS BUT WILL IMPRESS ON SPECIAL OCCASIONS.

Pumpkin Pie,
p. 20

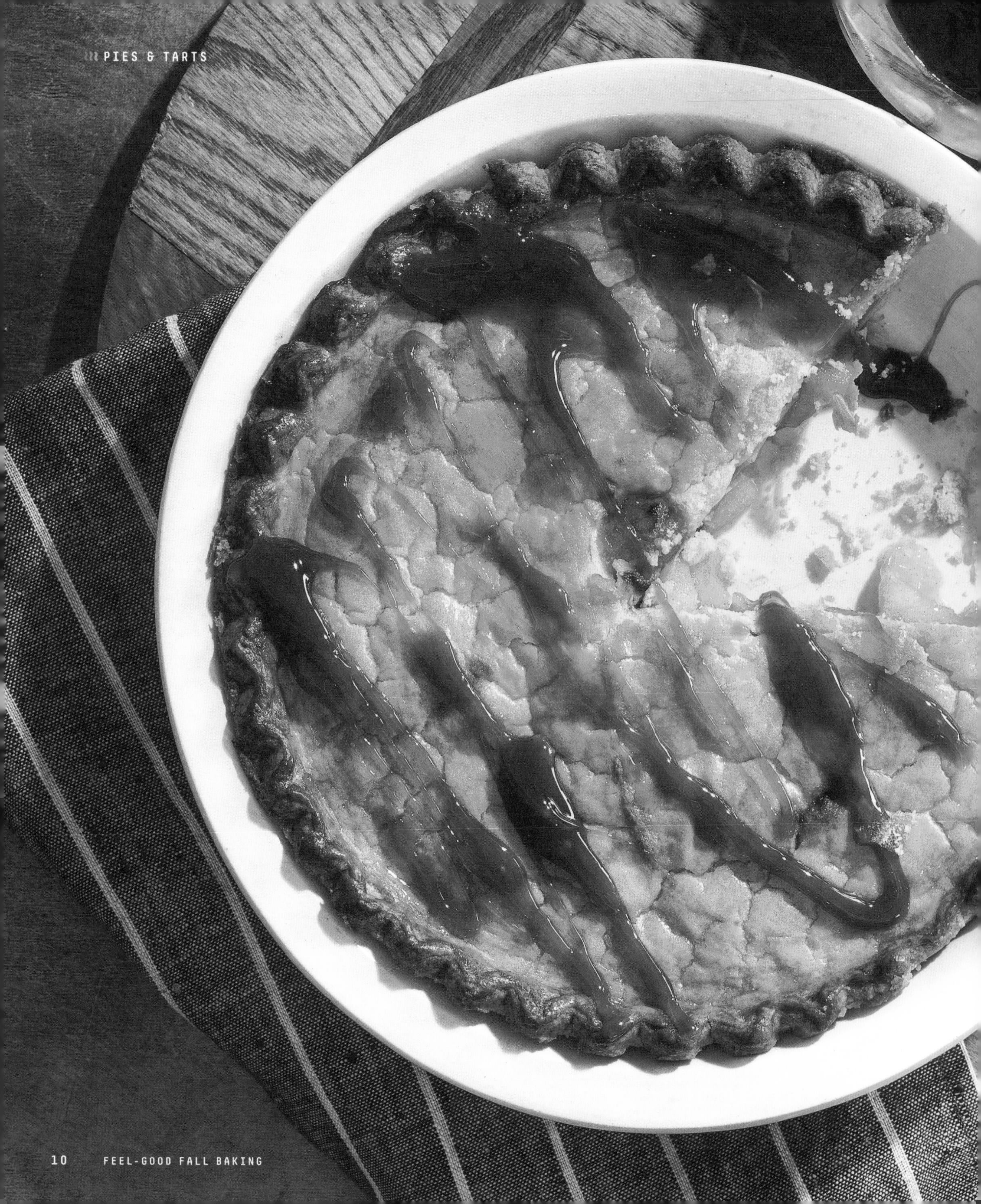

Caramel Apple Pie

Company-Worthy • Easy • Family Favorite

The yummy flavor of caramel apple shines through in this super-simple pie.

PREP *25 minutes*

TOTAL *1 hour 25 minutes; 2 hours inactive*

YIELD *8 servings*

Ingredients

- 1 (14.1-ounce) box refrigerated pie crust
- 1 cup caramel sauce, divided
- 4 tablespoons all-purpose flour, divided
- 6 apples, peeled, cored and sliced
- ½ cup brown sugar
- 1 teaspoon cinnamon
- 1 teaspoon milk
- 2 teaspoons sugar

Instructions

1 Heat oven to 400 F.

2 Arrange crust in pie pan.

3 In a small bowl, combine ½ cup caramel sauce with 2 tablespoons flour. Spread on bottom of pie crust.

4 In a large bowl, mix apples, brown sugar, cinnamon and remaining 2 tablespoons flour. Spoon over caramel in pie crust.

5 Place remaining crust over apples and crimp as desired. Brush with milk and sprinkle with sugar. Cut 4 slits in top of pie.

6 Bake for 60 to 65 minutes or until crust is browned. Cool on wire rack for 2 hours.

7 Drizzle with remaining ½ cup caramel sauce and serve.

Coconut Sweet Potato Pie With Marshmallow Meringue

All-American • Company-Worthy • Holiday Classic

The flavor of this pie is reminiscent of your grandmother's traditional sweet potato casserole.

PREP *35 minutes*

TOTAL *1 hour 40 minutes;*
3 hours inactive

YIELD *8 servings*

Pie

- ½ (14.1-ounce) package refrigerated pie crust
- 1 cup evaporated milk
- ¾ cup brown sugar, packed
- ¼ cup cream cheese, softened
- 2 cups cooked and mashed sweet potatoes
- 1 cup sweetened coconut
- 3 eggs, beaten
- 2 teaspoons lemon juice
- 2 teaspoons vanilla extract
- ¼ teaspoon salt
- ½ teaspoon cinnamon

Meringue

- ¾ cup sugar
- ⅓ cup water
- 4 egg whites, at room temperature
- ¼ teaspoon cream of tartar
- 1 (7-ounce) jar marshmallow creme
   Optional garnishes: mini marshmallows, sweetened shredded coconut

For the pie

1 Preheat oven to 425 F.

2 Roll out 1 pie crust to fit a 9-inch deep-dish pie plate. Transfer to pie plate. Trim crust to ½ inch beyond edge of plate; flute edges. Refrigerate until ready to use.

3 In a small saucepan, combine evaporated milk, brown sugar and cream cheese. Cook and stir until smooth. Transfer to a large bowl; cool 5 minutes.

4 Whisk in sweet potatoes, coconut, eggs, lemon juice, vanilla, salt and cinnamon. Pour into prepared crust.

5 Bake on lower oven rack for 10 to 15 minutes. Reduce heat to 325 F and bake an additional 40 to 50 minutes, until set. Cover edges with foil during last 15 minutes to prevent over-browning if necessary.

6 Cool on wire rack. Refrigerate for at least 3 hours before topping with meringue.

For the meringue

1 In a small saucepan over medium-high heat, combine sugar and water; using a pastry brush dipped in water, wash down sides of pan to eliminate sugar crystals. When mixture comes to a boil, stop brushing. Cook without stirring until a thermometer reads 240 F (soft-ball stage).

2 As sugar mixture cooks, preheat broiler. Using an electric mixer on medium speed, beat egg whites and cream of tartar until soft peaks form, and then gradually drizzle hot sugar mixture over egg whites; continue beating until stiff glossy peaks form.

3 In a separate large bowl, place marshmallow creme; fold in one-third of egg-white mixture, then fold in remaining mixture. If necessary, beat again until stiff glossy peaks form.

4 Spread meringue over pie; broil 4 to 6 inches from heat until slightly browned, 1 or 2 minutes. Garnish as desired. Cool on wire rack before serving. Store leftovers in refrigerator.

Apple Hand Pies

All-American • Company-Worthy • Family Favorite

Classic apple pie gets a redo in this tasty (and transportable!) version.

PREP *25 minutes*

TOTAL *45 minutes*

YIELD *8 servings*

Ingredients

- 2 cups peeled and diced apples
- 1 tablespoon brown sugar
- ½ teaspoon cinnamon
- 1 tablespoon lemon juice
- 1 (17.3-ounce) package frozen puff pastry, thawed
- 1 egg, beaten
   Sanding sugar

Instructions

1 Preheat oven to 400 F. Line 2 baking sheets with parchment paper.

2 In a large bowl, combine apples, brown sugar, cinnamon and lemon juice.

3 Lightly dust a work surface with flour. Unfold puff pastry sheets and use a rolling pin to smooth out sheets and remove perforations. Cut each sheet into 4 squares.

4 Spoon one-eighth of apple mixture into center of each pastry square, then fold pastry in half diagonally to form a triangle.

5 Using a fork, crimp edges of pastry. Cut 3 small slits in the tops of each pie.

6 Place pies on prepared baking sheets. Brush with egg wash and sprinkle with sugar.

7 Bake for 18 to 20 minutes or until golden and puffed.

8 Transfer to wire racks to cool.

A Family Favorite!

Apple
Hand Pies

TIP
Get creative with pie edges! Use your fingers to twist or pinch them, or try kitchen implements—a fork, tongs, a citrus reamer—to make patterns.

Chocolate Chip Pecan Pie

Almond Pear Tart

Company-Worthy • Easy

You can use canned pear halves in place of the poached pears.

PREP *15 minutes*

TOTAL *1 hour 10 minutes*

YIELD *8 servings*

Ingredients

- 6 tablespoons almond paste
- 2 teaspoons sugar
- 2 teaspoons flour
- 3 tablespoons butter, cubed, softened
- 1 egg
- 1 egg white, at room temperature
- 1½ teaspoons rum
- 1 prebaked (9-inch) pie crust, cooled
- 3 poached pears (See Oven Poached Vanilla Bean Pears, page 150.)

Instructions

1 Preheat oven to 375 F.

2 In bowl of an electric mixer, beat almond paste, sugar and flour until smooth.

3 Gradually beat in butter until mixture is smooth, then beat in egg, egg white and rum. Spread mixture evenly over bottom of pie crust.

4 Blot pears dry with paper towels. Halve, core, then cut into thin slices. Arrange evenly over filling.

5 Bake for 40 to 45 minutes, or until pears and filling have browned slightly. Cool on wire rack before serving.

Chocolate Chip Pecan Pie

Company-Worthy • Family Favorite

This sweet treat will be a hit at your table any night of the week.

PREP *15 minutes*

TOTAL *1 hour; 2 hours inactive*

YIELD *8 servings*

Ingredients

- 3 eggs
- ⅔ cup sugar
- ½ teaspoon salt
- ⅓ cup butter, melted
- 1 cup light corn syrup
- 1 cup pecan halves
- 1 cup semisweet chocolate chips
- 1 (9-inch) unbaked pie crust

Instructions

1 Preheat oven to 375 F.

2 In a medium bowl, using a hand mixer or whisk, beat eggs, sugar, salt, butter and corn syrup.

Apple Pie
With Streusel
Topping

3 Fold in pecans and chocolate chips. Pour mixture into pie crust.

4 Bake until set, 45 to 50 minutes. Cool on wire rack for 2 hours before serving.

Apple Pie With Streusel Topping

All-American • Easy • Family Favorite

The difference between a traditional apple pie and this one is the delicious crumb topping.

PREP *20 minutes*

TOTAL *1 hour 10 minutes;*
2 hours inactive

YIELD *8 servings*

Ingredients

- 8 cups peeled and sliced apples
- ½ cup sugar
- 1¼ cups flour, divided
- ½ teaspoon cinnamon
- 1 tablespoon lemon juice
- 1 (9-inch) pie crust
- ⅔ cup brown sugar
- ½ cup butter, softened

Instructions

1 Preheat oven to 400 F.

2 In a large bowl, combine apples, sugar, ¼ cup flour, cinnamon and lemon juice. Pour into pie crust.

3 In a medium bowl, stir together remaining 1 cup flour and brown sugar. Use pastry blender to cut butter into mixture until it resembles wet sand. Sprinkle evenly over top of pie.

4 Bake for 45 to 50 minutes or until crumb topping is browned and filling begins to bubble.

5 Cool on wire rack for 2 hours before serving.

A French Classic Made Easy

Rustic Pear Tart With Dried Cherries

Company-Worthy • Easy

This impressive dessert looks hard to make, but is super simple and filled with flavor.

PREP *20 minutes*

TOTAL *1 hour 5 minutes;*
2 hours inactive

YIELD *8 servings*

Ingredients

- ½ (14.1-ounce) box refrigerated pie crust
- 3 cups sliced pears
- ¼ cup dried cherries
- 1 teaspoon vanilla extract
- ¼ cup sugar
- 1 tablespoon cornstarch
- 1 teaspoon cinnamon
- ¼ cup chopped walnuts
- 1 egg white
- 1 tablespoon water

Instructions

1 Preheat oven to 375 F.

2 Line a baking sheet with parchment paper.

3 On a lightly floured surface, roll out pie crust into a 14-inch circle.

4 Transfer crust to baking sheet; set aside.

5 In a large bowl, combine pears, cherries, vanilla, sugar, cornstarch, cinnamon and walnuts.

6 Spoon pear mixture over pastry to within 2 inches of edge. Fold edges of pastry over filling, leaving center uncovered.

7 Beat egg white and water together and brush over folded pastry.

8 Bake for 35 to 40 minutes or until crust is golden and filling is bubbly.

9 Cool on wire rack for 2 hours before serving.

Black Bottom
Oatmeal Pie

Black Bottom Oatmeal Pie

Company-Worthy • Easy • Family Favorite

Oatmeal replaces pecans in this gooey pie, which will keep refrigerated for three days or at room temperature for two days.

PREP *15 minutes*

TOTAL *1 hour 15 minutes; 2 hours inactive*

YIELD *8 servings*

Ingredients

1½ cups old-fashioned oats

¼ cup heavy cream

4 ounces bittersweet chocolate, chopped

¾ cup light brown sugar

½ teaspoon salt

5 tablespoons butter, melted

1 cup dark corn syrup

1 teaspoon vanilla extract

2 teaspoons apple cider vinegar

4 eggs

1 prebaked (9-inch) pie crust

Instructions

1 Preheat oven to 350 F. Spread oats on a baking sheet and toast for 10 to 12 minutes, until golden brown.

2 Reduce heat to 325 F. In a heavy saucepan over medium-high heat, bring cream just to a boil. Remove from heat and add chocolate, stirring until melted.

3 Pour chocolate-cream mixture into pie crust. Place in freezer to firm.

4 In a large bowl, whisk together brown sugar, salt, butter, corn syrup, vanilla, apple cider vinegar and eggs. Stir in toasted oats. Pour mixture over chilled crust.

5 Bake for 50 to 55 minutes.

6 Cool on wire rack for 2 hours before serving.

Chocolate Chess Pie

Easy • Family Favorite

This sweet Southern favorite takes minimum effort but yields big results in chocolaty goodness!

PREP *15 minutes*

TOTAL *1 hour*

YIELD *8 servings*

Ingredients

½ (14.1-ounce) box refrigerated pie crust

¼ cup butter, melted

1½ cups sugar

¼ cup unsweetened cocoa powder

3 eggs

½ teaspoon vanilla extract

1 tablespoon cornmeal

    Garnish: whipped cream

Instructions

1 Preheat oven to 350 F.

2 On a lightly floured surface, roll out 1 pie crust.

3 Place crust in an ungreased 9-inch glass pie plate, pressing firmly against bottom and side. Trim any overhang; crimp edges.

4 Place in refrigerator while preparing filling.

5 In deep bowl, stir together melted butter, sugar and cocoa until blended. Add eggs and vanilla. Using a whisk, beat until mixture is blended and thickens. Stir in cornmeal just until combined; pour into crust.

6 Bake 40 to 45 minutes or until pie is set.

7 Cool completely. Serve at room temperature with a dollop of whipped cream.

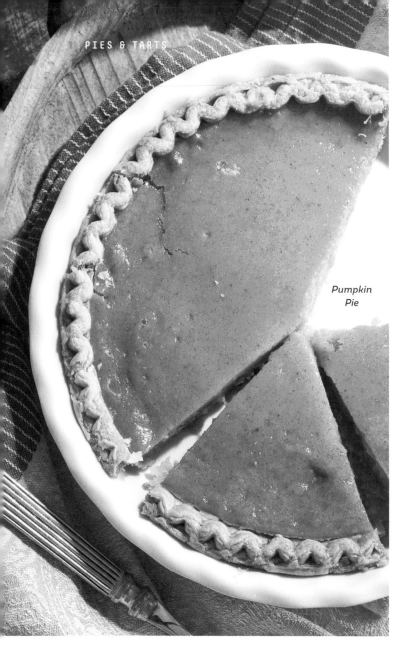

Pumpkin Pie

Instructions

1 Preheat oven to 425 F.

2 In a large bowl, combine sugar, pumpkin pie spice, salt, eggs, pumpkin puree and evaporated milk.

3 Pour into pie crust. Bake for 40 minutes or until knife inserted into center comes out clean.

4 Cool on wire rack for 2 hours before serving or refrigerating.

Peanut Butter Pie With Peanut Butter Cup Topping

All-American • Easy • Family Favorite

After you make and bake the crust, the rest of this decadent pie is a breeze to put together.

PREP *10 minutes*

TOTAL *20 minutes, 2 hours inactive*

YIELD *8 servings*

Ingredients

- 25   whole chocolate sandwich cookies, crushed
- ¼   cup butter, melted
- 8   ounces cream cheese, softened
- 1¼   cups creamy peanut butter
- 1   cup powdered sugar, divided
- 1½   teaspoons vanilla extract, divided
- 2   cups heavy cream, divided
- 2   tablespoons cocoa powder
-     Garnish: chopped peanut butter cups

Instructions

1 Preheat oven to 350 F.

2 In a large bowl, combine crushed cookies and melted butter.

3 Press mixture into a 9-inch pie plate and bake for 5 to 7 minutes.

4 Remove from oven and cool completely, about 30 minutes.

5 In a large bowl, using a hand mixer, beat cream cheese, peanut butter, ¾ cup powdered sugar and 1 teaspoon vanilla until smooth.

6 In another bowl, whip 1 cup cream until heavy peaks form. Fold into peanut butter mixture.

7 Pour mixture into cooled crust and refrigerate for 2 hours.

8 In a medium bowl, whip remaining cream until stiff peaks form. Fold in cocoa powder, remaining ¼ cup powdered sugar and remaining ½ teaspoon vanilla.

9 Spread cocoa mixture over refrigerated pie and top with chopped peanut butter cups, if desired.

10 Store in refrigerator.

Pumpkin Pie

All-American • Family Favorite • Holiday Classic

Nothing screams autumn like a big slice of pumpkin pie!

PREP *15 minutes*

TOTAL *1 hour; 2 hours inactive*

YIELD *8 servings*

Ingredients

- ¾   cup sugar
- 2   teaspoons pumpkin pie spice
- ½   teaspoon salt
- 2   eggs
- 1   (15-ounce) can pumpkin puree
- 1   (12-ounce) can evaporated milk
- 1   (9-inch) deep-dish pie crust, unbaked

TIP
You can substitute chopped Snickers, Peanut M&M's or dark chocolate peanut clusters for the peanut butter cups.

Peanut Butter
Pie With
Peanut Butter
Cup Topping

Southern Comfort Food in Every Bite

TIP
By baking the sweet potatoes instead of boiling them, the sugar in them will caramelize, giving you a sweeter, richer-tasting pie.

Traditional Sweet Potato Pie

Easy • Family Favorite

This heavenly pie is super rich and is a wonderful way to end any meal.

PREP *15 minutes*

TOTAL *1 hour 15 minutes;*
1 hour inactive

YIELD *8 servings*

Ingredients

- ¼ cup butter, melted
- ⅔ cup sugar
- ⅓ cup evaporated milk
- 2 eggs
- 1 teaspoon pumpkin pie spice
- ½ teaspoon vanilla extract
- ½ teaspoon salt
- 2 cups cooked and mashed sweet potatoes
- 1 (9-inch) premade pie crust
  Garnish: whipped cream, dusting of cinnamon

Instructions

1 Preheat oven to 350 F.

2 In a large bowl, whisk together butter and sugar. Stir in evaporated milk, eggs, pumpkin pie spice, vanilla and salt. Fold in sweet potatoes.

3 Pour into pie crust and bake for 55 to 60 minutes or until a toothpick inserted in center comes out clean.

4 Cool on wire rack for 1 hour before serving.

5 Garnish with whipped cream and cinnamon, if desired.

Simple Tarte Tatin

Company-Worthy • Easy • Family Favorite

Caramel sauce makes this classic dessert a cinch to put together.

PREP *20 minutes*

TOTAL *1 hour*

YIELD *6 servings*

Ingredients

- 1 sheet frozen puff pastry, thawed
- 1 egg, beaten
- 1 cup ground almonds
- 1 teaspoon cinnamon
- 2 apples, thinly sliced
- 2 pears, thinly sliced
- 1 tablespoon lemon juice
- 2 tablespoons brown sugar
- 3 tablespoons caramel sauce

Instructions

1 Preheat oven to 375 F. Line a baking sheet with parchment paper and spread puff pastry on it. Generously brush with egg.

2 In a medium bowl, stir almonds and cinnamon. Sprinkle evenly over center of pastry.

3 In another bowl, toss apples, pears and lemon juice. Arrange in a pretty pattern on top of almonds. Sprinkle with brown sugar.

4 Bake for 30 to 35 minutes until pastry is puffed and golden.

5 Warm caramel sauce in microwave. Brush over tart and serve while still warm.

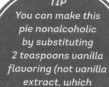

TIP
You can make this pie nonalcoholic by substituting 2 teaspoons vanilla flavoring (not vanilla extract, which contains alcohol), for the bourbon.

Bourbon Pecan Pie

Company-Worthy • Easy • Holiday Classic

The bourbon in this pie helps to bring out the flavor of the pecans.

PREP *15 minutes*

TOTAL *50 minutes, 2 hours inactive*

YIELD *8 servings*

Ingredients

- ½ cup sugar
- ½ cup brown sugar
- 3 tablespoons butter, melted
- ½ cup light corn syrup
- 3 eggs, beaten
- 2 tablespoons bourbon
- 2 cups pecan halves
- 1 (9-inch) deep-dish pie crust, unbaked

Instructions

1 Preheat oven to 375 F.

2 In a large bowl, combine both sugars, butter, corn syrup, eggs and bourbon.

3 Fold in pecans. Pour into pie crust.

4 Bake for 10 minutes, then reduce heat to 350 F and bake an additional 25 to 30 minutes or until set.

5 Cool on wire rack for 2 hours before serving.

An Adults-Only Pecan Pie!

Bourbon Pecan Pie

Cakes & Cheesecakes

NOTHING SAYS CELEBRATION LIKE A CAKE! WHETHER YOU HAVE A HANKERING FOR SOMETHING CHOCOLATE OR YOU'RE MORE OF A CHEESECAKE PERSON, WE HAVE A RECIPE FOR YOUR PERFECT ENDING.

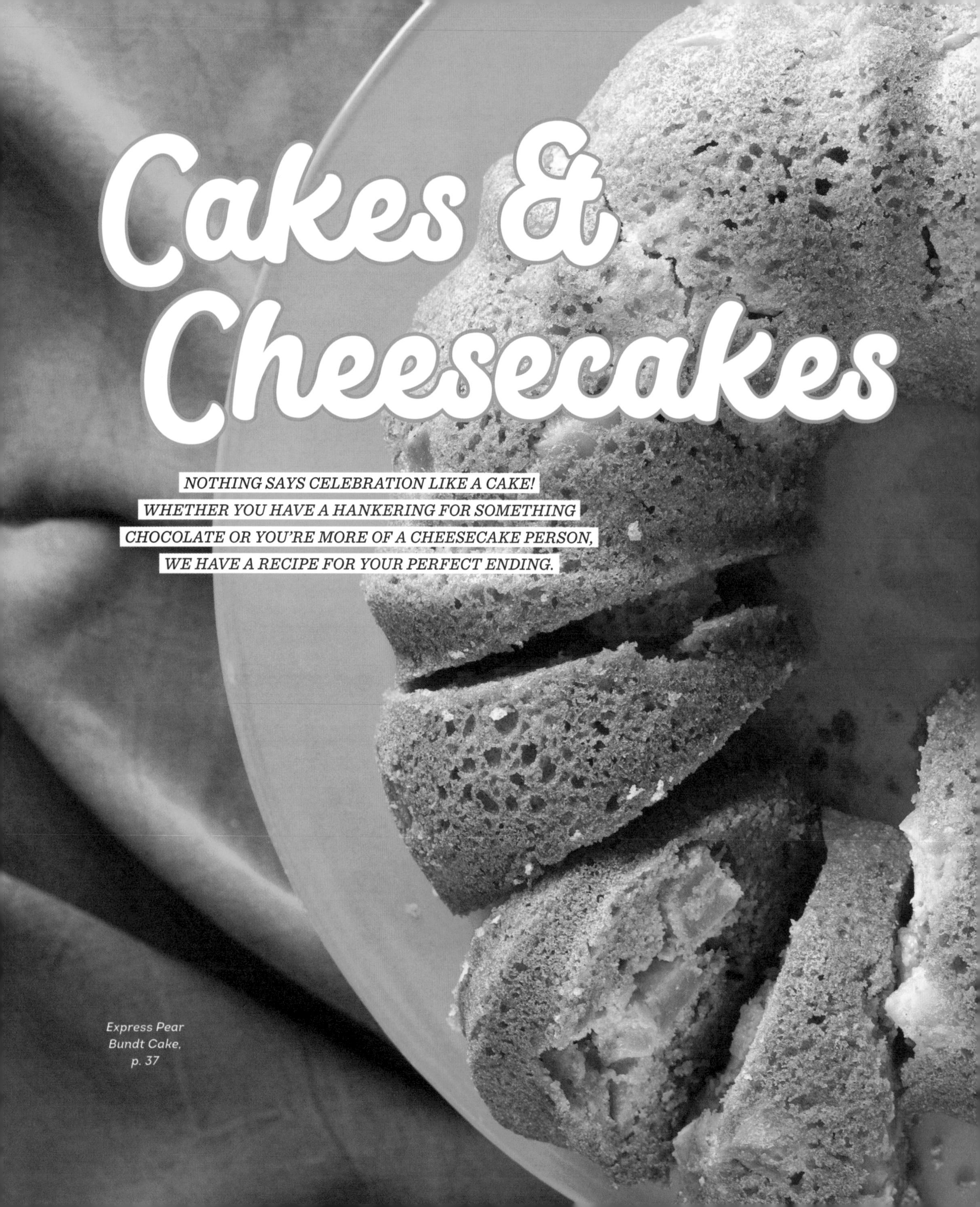

Express Pear
Bundt Cake,
p. 37

TIP
Place the cake on a big platter before icing, so drips don't get all over your counter.

Hot Cocoa Bundt Cake With Marshmallow Icing

All-American • Family Favorite • Holiday Classic

This cake tastes just like hot cocoa!

PREP *30 minutes*

TOTAL *4 hours; 2 hours 15 minutes inactive*

YIELD *12 servings*

Ingredients

2	teaspoons unsweetened cocoa
1	cup water
¾	cup butter, cubed
¾	cup vegetable oil
⅔	cup semisweet chocolate chips
1½	cups sugar
3	eggs, at room temperature
3	cups all-purpose flour
¾	cup sweet ground chocolate and cocoa powder*
2½	teaspoons baking soda
½	teaspoon salt
¾	cup buttermilk
1	tablespoon vanilla extract
1	cup marshmallow creme

Note: You can find sweet ground chocolate and cocoa powder in the hot-beverage aisle.

Instructions

1 Heat oven to 350 F. Grease a 12-cup Bundt pan; dust with cocoa.

2 In a large saucepan, stir together water, butter, oil and chocolate chips. Cook over low heat 6 to 8 minutes, stirring constantly, until chips are melted and mixture is smooth.

3 Stir in sugar, let cool for 5 minutes. Whisk in eggs, one at a time, until just blended.

4 In a medium bowl, whisk together flour, ground chocolate and cocoa powder, baking soda and salt. Add to chocolate mixture, alternating with buttermilk, stirring just until blended. Add vanilla.

5 Pour batter into prepared pan. Bake 45 to 50 minutes, or until toothpick inserted in center comes out clean.

6 Cool cake in pan for 15 minutes, then invert it onto cooling rack. Let cool completely, about 2 hours.

7 Place marshmallow creme into quart-size zip-close bag; seal bag. Snip off one lower corner of bag about ½-inch deep; drizzle marshmallow creme on cake.

Applesauce Cake With Caramel Frosting

All-American • Easy • Family Favorite

The rich fall flavors of this moist cake perfectly complement the caramel frosting.

PREP *40 minutes*

TOTAL *1 hour 10 minutes; 1 hour inactive*

YIELD *12 servings*

Cake

- ½ cup butter, softened
- 1 cup sugar
- ½ cup dark brown sugar
- 2 eggs
- 1 teaspoon vanilla extract
- 1½ cups applesauce
- 2 cups all-purpose flour
- ¼ teaspoon baking powder
- 1½ teaspoons baking soda
- 1 teaspoon apple pie spice
- ½ teaspoon ground cloves
- ½ teaspoon ground nutmeg
- 1 teaspoon salt

Frosting

- ½ cup butter
- 1 cup dark brown sugar, lightly packed
- ½ teaspoon salt
- ½ cup whole milk
- 1 teaspoon vanilla extract
- 2 cups powdered sugar, sifted
- ½ cup chopped walnuts, toasted

For the cake

1 Preheat oven to 350 F. Coat a 9-inch square baking pan with cooking spray.

2 In bowl of electric mixer, cream butter and both sugars until fluffy. Beat in eggs one at a time. Add vanilla and applesauce.

3 Add flour, baking powder, baking soda, spices and salt. Mix until just incorporated.

4 Pour batter into prepared pan and bake until a toothpick inserted in center comes out clean, about 35 to 45 minutes. Let cake cool completely.

For the frosting

1 In a medium saucepan over medium-low heat, melt butter. Whisk in brown sugar, salt and milk. Bring to a boil and cook for 2 minutes, stirring continuously. Remove from heat and cool for 10 to 15 minutes.

2 Add vanilla and powdered sugar. Whisk until smooth.

3 Once cake is completely cool, frost cake. Sprinkle with toasted walnuts.

Pecan Pie Cheesecake

Company-Worthy • Family Favorite

Now you don't have to decide between the two most delicious desserts ever. This amazing recipe combines the two!

PREP *30 minutes*

TOTAL *2 hours 10 minutes; 6 hours inactive*

YIELD *10 servings*

Crust

- 1 sleeve (9 large rectangles) graham crackers, finely crushed
- 5 tablespoons melted butter
- ¼ cup brown sugar

Filling

- 3 (8-ounce) packages cream cheese, softened
- 1 cup brown sugar
- 3 eggs
- ¼ cup sour cream
- 2 tablespoons all-purpose flour
- 1 teaspoon vanilla extract
- ¼ teaspoon salt

Topping

- 1 cup pecan butter
- 1¾ cups chopped pecans

For the crust

1 Preheat oven to 325 F. Coat an 8-inch springform pan with cooking spray.

2 In a large bowl, mix together graham cracker crumbs, melted butter and brown sugar. Press mixture into prepared pan.

3 Bake for 10 minutes.

For the filling

1 In the bowl of an electric mixer, beat cream cheese and brown sugar. Add in eggs, one at a time, mixing to incorporate after each addition. Beat in sour cream, flour, vanilla and salt.

2 Pour filling over crust. Wrap bottom of pan in aluminum foil and place on a baking sheet.

3 Bake until center of cheesecake is slightly jiggly, about 1 hour 30 minutes.

4 Turn off heat, prop open oven door, and let cheesecake cool in oven, 1 hour. Remove from oven and take off aluminum foil. Allow to cool to room temperature then refrigerate at least 5 hours.

For the topping

Before serving, spread pecan butter over top and sprinkle with chopped pecans.

TIP
Store pecans in an airtight container in your refrigerator.

Pecan Pie Cheesecake

Cider Pound
Cake

Cider Pound Cake

Company-Worthy • Easy • Family Favorite

Sparkling apple cider really intensifies this cake's flavor.

PREP *20 minutes*

TOTAL *1 hour 10 minutes;*
20 minutes inactive

YIELD *12 servings*

Cake

- 2 cups butter, softened
- 2 cups sugar
- 6 eggs
- 3¼ cups all-purpose flour
- ¼ teaspoon salt
- ½ cup sparkling apple cider

Icing

- 1½ cups powdered sugar
- 1 teaspoon vanilla extract
- 3 tablespoons sparkling cider

For the cake

1 Preheat oven to 350 F. Coat a 10-inch tube pan with cooking spray.

2 In the bowl of an electric mixer, cream butter and sugar until fluffy.

3 Add eggs, one at a time, beating well after each addition.

4 In another bowl, whisk together flour and salt; add one-third to butter mixture, followed by one-third of cider; repeat two more times, beating well after each addition.

5 Pour batter into prepared pan.

6 Bake 1 hour 10 minutes or until a toothpick inserted in cake comes out clean.

7 Cool in pan on wire rack for 20 minutes, then invert cake onto a serving platter.

For the icing

1 In a medium bowl, add sugar. Slowly whisk in vanilla and cider until smooth.

2 Drizzle or spoon icing over cooled cake.

Moist Honey Cake

All-American • Easy

This rich cake can be made ahead and enjoyed for a week.

PREP *20 minutes*

TOTAL *1 hour 40 minutes*

YIELD *10 servings*

Ingredients

- 3½ cups all-purpose flour
- 1 tablespoon baking powder
- 1 teaspoon baking soda
- ½ teaspoon salt
- 4 teaspoons ground cinnamon
- ½ teaspoon ground cloves
- 1 cup vegetable oil
- 1 cup honey
- 1½ cups sugar
- ½ cup brown sugar
- 3 eggs
- 1 teaspoon vanilla extract
- 1 cup brewed coffee
- ½ cup fresh orange juice
- ¼ cup bourbon
- ½ cup sliced almonds

Instructions

1 Preheat oven to 350 F. Grease a 10-inch tube pan.

2 In a large bowl, combine flour, baking powder, baking soda, salt and spices.

3 In a medium bowl, using a hand mixer at low speed, mix oil, honey, both sugars, eggs, vanilla, coffee, orange juice and bourbon.

4 Make a well in center of dry ingredients and add oil-honey mixture. Gradually blend together until incorporated.

5 Place batter into prepared pan, and then sprinkle almonds on top. Bake for 60 to 70 minutes.

6 Let cake stand for 15 minutes, then invert it onto a serving platter to cool completely.

Caramel Cheesecake

All-American • Company-Worthy

Luscious caramel makes the rich cheesecake filling
that much better!

PREP *35 minutes*

TOTAL *1 hour 10 minutes; 7 hours inactive*

YIELD *8 servings*

Crust

- 2 cups graham cracker crumbs
- ⅓ cup sugar
- 1 teaspoon salt
- 1 teaspoon cinnamon
- 10 tablespoons unsalted butter, melted

Filling

- 4 8-ounce packages full-fat cream cheese, at room temperature
- ½ cup sour cream
- 1⅓ cups granulated sugar
- 2 teaspoons vanilla extract
- 3 tablespoons all-purpose flour
- 3 eggs, at room temperature

Sauce

- 2 tablespoons unsalted butter
- ¾ cup heavy cream
- ½ cup brown sugar
- ⅛ teaspoon salt
- 1 teaspoon vanilla extract

For the crust

1 Preheat oven to 350 F. Coat a 9-inch springform pan with cooking spray.

2 In a medium bowl, stir graham cracker crumbs, sugar, salt, cinnamon and butter together until combined.

3 Press into bottom of springform pan.

4 Bake for 10 minutes.

5 Remove from oven; lower oven temperature to 325 F.

For the filling

1 Using an electric mixer at medium speed, beat cream cheese until smooth. Add sour cream, sugar and vanilla and mix until combined.

2 Add flour, then eggs, one at a time, and beat until fully incorporated. Do not overmix. Pour batter into prepared springform pan.

3 Place a roasting pan on lower rack of oven and fill with boiling water.

4 Place cheesecake on upper rack of oven and bake for 1 hour 10 minutes.

5 Turn off oven and let cheesecake cool for 30 minutes without opening oven door. Then crack open oven door and let cheesecake continue to cool for an additional 30 minutes.

6 Place on wire rack to finish cooling. When it reaches room temperature, put in refrigerator to chill an additional 5 hours.

For the sauce

1 Before serving, in a medium saucepan over medium-low heat, combine butter, heavy cream, brown sugar and salt. Cook, whisking continuously, until thickened. Add vanilla and cook for 1 minute.

2 Pour caramel over cheesecake and serve.

You'll Be Tempted to Skip Dinner!

*Applesauce
Cupcakes*

Express Pear Bundt Cake

Applesauce Cupcakes

All-American • Easy • Family Favorite

The applesauce in these cupcakes makes them extra moist and tender.

PREP *35 minutes*

TOTAL *1 hour; 30 minutes inactive*

YIELD *24 servings*

Cupcakes

1¼ cups sugar

½ cup butter, softened

2 eggs

1½ cups applesauce

2½ cups all-purpose flour

1 teaspoon cinnamon

1 teaspoon baking powder

½ teaspoon baking soda

½ teaspoon salt

Frosting

½ cup butter

4 cups powdered sugar

2 teaspoons vanilla extract

¼ cup half-and-half

Garnish

Apple slices sprinkled with lemon juice

For the cupcakes

1 Preheat oven to 350 F. Grease two 12-cup muffin tins.

2 In large bowl, using an electric hand mixer on medium speed, cream sugar and butter until fluffy. Add eggs and applesauce; beat until combined.

3 On low speed, beat in flour, cinnamon, baking powder, baking soda and salt. Spoon batter into muffin cups.

4 Bake 30 to 35 minutes or until toothpick inserted in center comes out clean. Remove from muffin tins and cool completely on wire rack.

For the frosting

1 In a medium saucepan over medium-low heat, melt butter. Cook 5 to 6 minutes, stirring constantly, until butter just begins to turn light brown. (Be careful not to let it burn.) Remove from heat and let cool.

2 Using a hand mixer, beat in powdered sugar, vanilla and half-and-half until smooth. Add more half-and-half if needed to achieve a spreadable consistency. When cupcakes are completely cooled, frost. Garnish with apple slices.

TIP
If the cake doesn't come out right away, let it sit for about 15 minutes so gravity can do the job.

Express Pear Bundt Cake

All-American • Easy • Family Favorite

A cake mix lets you throw this super-simple dessert together in five minutes—and with pears replacing the oil, it's very low in fat, with added fiber.

PREP *5 minutes*

TOTAL *55 minutes*

YIELD *10 servings*

Ingredients

1 (15 oz.) can pear halves in light syrup

1 (15.25-ounce) box white cake mix

1 whole egg

2 egg whites

Instructions

1 Preheat oven to 350 F. Grease a 10-inch Bundt pan.

2 Drain pears; reserve syrup. Mash pears with fork, leaving a few small chunks.

3 Transfer pears to a large bowl. Add reserved syrup, cake mix, egg and egg whites.

4 Using a hand mixer at low speed, beat mixture for 30 seconds to incorporate ingredients, then on high speed for another 3 minutes. Pour batter into prepared pan.

5 Bake for 50 to 55 minutes or until a toothpick inserted in center comes out clean.

Carrot Cake With Cream Cheese Frosting

All-American • Company-Worthy • Family Favorite

Four layers of moist carrot cake are filled and topped with the creamiest cream cheese frosting.

PREP *1 hour*

TOTAL *1 hour, 30 minutes; 1 hour inactive*

YIELD *10 servings*

Cake

- 1 cup canola oil
- 1½ cups brown sugar
- ½ cup sugar
- 3 eggs, beaten
- 2½ cups all-purpose flour
- 1 teaspoon baking soda
- 1 tablespoon ground cinnamon
- 1 teaspoon salt
- 4 medium carrots, grated

Frosting

- 2 (8-ounce packages) cream cheese, softened
- ½ cup butter, softened
- 1 teaspoon vanilla extract
- 1 tablespoon heavy cream
- 4½ cups powdered sugar

For the cake

1 Preheat oven to 300 F. Grease two 8-inch round cake pans.

2 In the bowl of an electric mixer on medium speed, combine oil and both sugars. Beat in eggs.

3 Gradually add flour, baking soda, cinnamon and salt. Fold in grated carrots.

4 Pour batter into prepared pans.

5 Bake for 32 to 35 minutes.

6 Remove from oven and cool on wire rack for 1 hour.

For the frosting

1 In the bowl of an electric mixer on medium speed, beat cream cheese and butter until smooth.

2 Stir in vanilla and cream and mix for 30 seconds. On low speed, slowly add powdered sugar and beat until frosting is a spreadable consistency.

To assemble

1 Cut each cake in half horizontally to create four thin layers.

2 Place one layer on a cake stand, cover it with cream cheese frosting, and then place another layer over it. Repeat with all four layers.

3 Frost outside of cake.

Tangy and Delicious!

TIP
For a quicker version, bake in a 13x9-inch pan for 40 to 45 minutes. The proportion of frosting to cake will be lower, but it will still taste amazing!

TIP
Even pans advertised as leakproof can have "accidents." Prevent a mess by placing the cheesecake on a baking sheet before putting it in the oven.

*Pumpkin Pie
Cheesecake*

Two Favorites in One!

Pumpkin Pie Cheesecake

All-American • Company-Worthy • Holiday Classic

Cheesecake and pumpkin pie lovers will both get to enjoy their favorite flavors in this dessert.

PREP *25 minutes*

TOTAL *1 hour 15 minutes; 5 hours inactive*

YIELD *12 servings*

Crust

- 2 cups graham cracker crumbs
- 3 tablespoons butter, melted
- 2 tablespoons sugar

Filling

- 2 (8-ounce) packages cream cheese, softened
- ¾ cup light brown sugar
- 3 eggs
- 1 (15-ounce) can pumpkin puree
- 1 tablespoon flour
- 2 teaspoons vanilla extract
- 1½ teaspoons pumpkin pie spice

Topping

- 1 cup pumpkin puree
- ½ cup sugar
- 1 cup chopped pecans

For the crust

1 Preheat oven to 350 F. Combine graham cracker crumbs, butter and sugar in a medium bowl.

2 Press into bottom of 9-inch springform pan. Set aside.

For the filling

1 In the bowl of an electric mixer on medium speed, beat cream cheese and brown sugar until fluffy.

2 Add eggs one at a time, then beat in pumpkin puree, flour, vanilla and pumpkin pie spice.

3 Pour into crust and bake 50 minutes, or until center is almost set.

4 Turn off oven but leave cheesecake in oven 1 hour. Remove and run small knife around edge of cheesecake to loosen.

5 Cool in pan on wire rack until it reaches room temperature, then refrigerate at least 5 hours.

For the topping

1 In a small bowl, beat together pumpkin puree and sugar.

2 Spread on top of cheesecake and sprinkle with chopped pecans.

Dutch Apple Loaf Cake

Easy • Family Favorite

Enjoy this cake with a cup of hot tea for an afternoon pick-me-up.

PREP *15 minutes*

TOTAL *1 hour 15 minutes*

YIELD *16 servings*

Topping

- ¼ cup sugar
- ¼ cup all-purpose flour
- 2 teaspoons ground cinnamon
- ¼ cup cold butter, cubed

Cake

- ½ cup butter, softened
- 1 cup sugar
- 2 eggs, at room temperature
- ¼ cup buttermilk
- 1 teaspoon vanilla extract
- 2 cups all-purpose flour
- 1½ teaspoons baking powder
- ¼ teaspoon baking soda
- ½ teaspoon salt
- 2 cups diced apples
- ½ cup chopped walnuts

For the topping

In a small bowl, combine sugar, flour and cinnamon. Cut in butter until mixture resembles coarse crumbs. Set aside.

For the cake

1 Preheat oven to 350 F. Grease a 9x5-inch loaf pan.

2 In the bowl of an electric mixer on medium speed, cream butter and sugar until fluffy. Add eggs, one at a time, beating well after each addition.

3 Beat in buttermilk and vanilla. At low speed, gradually add flour, baking powder, baking soda and salt.

4 Fold in apples and walnuts. Pour into prepared pan and sprinkle topping over batter.

5 Bake for 55 to 60 minutes or until a toothpick inserted in center comes out clean. Cool for 10 minutes before removing from pan to a wire rack.

Sweet Potato Cupcakes With Chocolate Frosting

Family Favorite • Holiday Classic

Using pureed sweet potato creates an incredibly moist batter!

PREP *20 minutes*

TOTAL *40 minutes*

YIELD *12 servings*

Ingredients

- ½ cup coconut oil or butter
- ½ cup light brown sugar
- ½ cup sugar
- 1 egg
- 1 egg yolk
- ½ teaspoon vanilla extract
- ½ cup cooked and pureed sweet potato
- ⅔ cup all-purpose flour
- ⅔ cup white whole-wheat pastry flour
- ¾ teaspoon baking powder
- ¼ teaspoon baking soda
- ¼ teaspoon salt
- ½ teaspoon cinnamon
- ¼ cup milk
- 1 (12-ounce) can chocolate frosting

Instructions

1 Preheat oven to 350 F. Line a muffin pan with 12 paper liners and set aside.

2 In the bowl of an electric mixer on medium speed, cream coconut oil with sugars. Stir in egg, egg yolk, vanilla and sweet potato. Scrape sides and whip until light and fluffy.

3 In another large bowl, using a fork or whisk, stir together flours, baking powder, baking soda, salt and cinnamon.

4 With electric mixer on low speed, alternate mixing in dry ingredients with milk, starting and ending with dry. Once ingredients are all incorporated, mix batter together by hand to ensure everything is mixed evenly.

5 Spoon into prepared muffin pan. Place in oven. Reduce temperature to 325 F. Bake 18 to 22 minutes or until inserted toothpick comes out clean.

6 Cool on wire rack. Frost cooled cupcakes with chocolate frosting. (We piped frosting with a star tip.)

TIP
Whole-wheat pastry flour will give your baked goods a nutritional boost, but you can sub regular all-purpose flour.

A Great Pairing!

AKA Monkey Bread

Caramel Pull Apart Cake

Caramel Pull Apart Cake

All-American • Easy • Family Favorite

While this cake bakes, it creates a delicious, sumptuous sauce that your family will love to get their hands on!

PREP *10 minutes*

TOTAL *40 minutes*

YIELD *10 servings*

Ingredients

- 2 (12-ounce) cans refrigerator biscuits, quartered
- 1 cup brown sugar
- ½ cup heavy whipping cream
- 1 teaspoon cinnamon

Instructions

1 Preheat oven to 350 F. Coat a 10-inch Bundt pan with cooking spray.

2 Arrange biscuit pieces evenly in prepared pan.

3 In a small bowl, stir together brown sugar, cream and cinnamon. Pour over biscuits.

4 Bake 25 to 30 minutes. Let cool slightly, then place on a serving plate.

Spice Cake With Maple Frosting

All-American • Easy • Family Favorite

This sweet maple frosting is delectable and pairs perfectly with the apple pie spice flavor.

PREP *25 minutes*

TOTAL *1 hour; 10 minutes inactive*

YIELD *16 servings*

Cake

- 2 cups flour
- 2 tablespoons cornstarch
- 1 tablespoon baking powder
- ½ teaspoon salt
- 2 tablespoons apple pie spice
- 1 cup butter, softened
- 2 cups light brown sugar
- 3 eggs
- 1 tablespoon vanilla extract
- 1 cup milk

Frosting

- 1 cup butter, softened
- ½ cup maple syrup
- 1 tablespoon vanilla extract
- 3½ cups powdered sugar

For the cake

1 Preheat oven to 350 F. Grease and flour two 9-inch round cake pans.

2 In a medium bowl, mix flour, cornstarch, baking powder, salt and apple pie spice. Set aside.

3 In the bowl of an electric mixer on medium speed, beat butter and brown sugar until light and fluffy. Beat in eggs, one at a time. Stir in vanilla.

4 On low speed, gradually beat in flour mixture alternating with milk until just blended. Do not overbeat. Pour batter into prepared pans.

5 Bake 30 minutes, or until toothpick inserted in center comes out clean.

6 Cool in pans 10 minutes. Remove from pans; cool completely on wire rack.

For the frosting

1 In the bowl of an electric mixer on medium speed, beat butter, maple syrup and vanilla until light and fluffy. Slowly add powdered sugar and beat well.

2 Place one cake layer on serving platter. Spread with one-third of frosting. Top with second cake layer. Spread remaining frosting on top and sides.

TIP
Make sure you put the same amount of batter in each cupcake cup to ensure they're all done at the same time.

Pumpkin Spice Cupcakes With Cream Cheese Frosting

All-American • Company-Worthy • Family Favorite

Use brick cream cheese when baking, since it's thicker than what comes in a tub.

PREP *30 minutes*

TOTAL *1 hour; 35 minutes inactive*

YIELD *12 servings*

Cupcakes

- 1½ cups all-purpose flour
- 1½ teaspoons pumpkin pie spice
- 1 teaspoon baking powder
- ½ teaspoon baking soda
- ¼ teaspoon salt
- 1 cup pure pumpkin
- 2 tablespoons molasses
- 1 teaspoon vanilla extract
- ½ cup butter, softened
- ¾ cup sugar
- 2 eggs

Frosting

- 4 ounces cream cheese, softened
- 2 tablespoons butter, softened
- 1 teaspoon vanilla extract
- 2 cups powdered sugar
- 1 teaspoon pumpkin pie spice

Garnish

- Pumpkin pie spice

For the cupcakes

1 Heat oven to 350 F. Line a muffin pan with 12 paper liners.

2 In a medium bowl, stir together flour, pumpkin pie spice, baking powder, baking soda and salt.

3 In another bowl, combine pumpkin, molasses and vanilla.

4 In the bowl of an electric mixer on medium speed, beat butter and sugar until fluffy. Beat in eggs, one at a time.

5 At low speed, add one-third of dry ingredients, then one-third of pumpkin mixture. Repeat two times, beating until batter is just combined.

6 Spoon batter into muffin cups and bake 25 to 30 minutes, or until toothpick inserted in center comes out clean.

7 Transfer to wire rack; let cool 5 minutes before removing cupcakes from pan. Let cool 30 minutes before frosting.

For the frosting

1 In the bowl of an electric mixer on medium speed, beat cream cheese and butter until fluffy. Add vanilla; gradually beat in sugar and pumpkin pie spice and beat until frosting is fluffy. Frost cupcakes; sprinkle with pumpkin pie spice.

TIP
Pro bakers recommend nonstick Bundt pans made of aluminum or coated steel. Avoid silicone ones—they make it easy for the batter to spill.

Apple Bundt Cake

All-American • Easy • Family Favorite

Granny Smith apples give this cake a sweet-tart flavor.

PREP *15 minutes*

TOTAL *1 hour 25 minutes; 1 hour, 20 minutes inactive*

YIELD *12 servings*

Ingredients

- 2 cups sugar
- 1½ cups vegetable oil
- 2 teaspoons vanilla extract

- 3 eggs
- 3 cups all-purpose flour
- 1 teaspoon baking soda
- 1 teaspoon cinnamon
- 1 teaspoon salt
- 3 medium Granny Smith apples, peeled, cored and cut into bite-size chunks

Instructions

1 Preheat oven to 325 F. Grease a 9-inch Bundt pan.

2 In the bowl of an electric mixer on medium speed, beat sugar and oil until fluffy. Add vanilla, then eggs, one at a time.

3 On low speed, gradually mix in flour, baking soda, cinnamon and salt just until incorporated. Fold in apples.

4 Pour batter into prepared Bundt pan.

5 Bake for 65 to 70 minutes, or until a toothpick inserted in center comes out clean.

6 Cool for 20 minutes in pan, then invert onto a serving dish to cool completely, about 1 hour.

A Good Reason to Go Apple-Picking!

TIP
For an Instagram-worthy frosted cake, refrigerate it before slicing, and use a knife dipped in hot water and then quickly dried.

Gingerbread Cake
With Cream Cheese Frosting

Company-Worthy • Family Favorite • Holiday Classic

This wonderfully spiced cake is even better when enjoyed the next day!

PREP *30 minutes*

TOTAL *1 hour 5 minutes; 1 hour inactive*

YIELD *9 servings*

Cake

- ¾ cup boiling water
- ½ teaspoon baking soda
- ⅔ cup molasses
- ¾ cup sugar
- 1⅔ cups all-purpose flour
- 2 teaspoons ground ginger
- 1 teaspoon cinnamon
- ¼ teaspoon nutmeg
- ⅛ teaspoon cloves
- ½ teaspoon baking powder
- ¼ teaspoon salt
- ⅓ cup vegetable oil
- 2 eggs

Frosting

- 1 (8-ounce) package cream cheese, softened
- ⅓ cup butter, softened
- 1 teaspoon vanilla extract
- 2 cups powdered sugar

For the cake

1 Preheat oven to 350 F. Grease a 9-inch square pan.

2 In a medium ceramic or glass mixing bowl, stir together boiling water and baking soda. Add molasses and sugar, whisking until well-combined and sugar has dissolved.

3 In a large mixing bowl, combine flour, ginger, cinnamon, nutmeg, cloves, baking powder and salt.

4 Whisk vegetable oil and eggs into molasses mixture, then slowly add wet mixture to dry ingredients until thoroughly blended.

5 Pour batter into prepared pan. Bake 30 to 35 minutes, or until a toothpick inserted in center comes out clean.

6 Cool 5 minutes, then run a knife around edge of cake. Cool on a wire rack for 1 hour.

For the frosting

1 In the bowl of an electric mixer fitted with a paddle attachment, whip together cream cheese and butter until pale and fluffy.

2 Add vanilla and powdered sugar and beat until well combined and spreadable. Frost cake and serve.

> **TIP**
> Most recipes that call for a Bundt pan can also be baked in two 9-inch round pans or one 13x9-inch rectangular pan.

Chai Bundt Cake

Company-Worthy • Family Favorite

Tea fans will love this aromatic cake.

PREP *15 minutes*

TOTAL *50 minutes*

YIELD *10 servings*

Ingredients

2 tablespoons chai tea blend
2 tablespoons boiling water
2¼ cups all-purpose flour
4 teaspoons baking powder
1 teaspoon salt
1½ cups sugar
2 teaspoons pumpkin pie spice
4 eggs
1½ cups milk
1 cup butter, melted
2 teaspoons vanilla extract

Instructions

1 Preheat oven to 350 F. Grease a 10-inch Bundt pan.
2 Brew tea: Pour boiling water over chai. Let steep for 5 minutes.
3 Meanwhile, in a large bowl, stir together flour, baking powder, salt, sugar and pumpkin pie spice. Make a well in center of mixture, then add eggs, milk, butter, vanilla and brewed chai.
4 Whisk in wet ingredients until smooth. Pour into prepared Bundt pan.
5 Bake for 30 to 35 minutes. Remove from oven and immediately invert onto rack. Let cool for 10 minutes, then lift off pan.
6 Let cool completely before serving.

Kentucky Butter Cake

Company-Worthy • Family Favorite

Introduce this classic Southern dessert to your family and friends.

PREP *20 minutes*

TOTAL *1 hour, 20 minutes*

YIELD *12 servings*

Cake

3 cups all-purpose flour
1 teaspoon baking powder
½ teaspoon baking soda
1 teaspoon salt
2 teaspoons vanilla extract
1 cup buttermilk
1 cup butter, softened
2 cups sugar
4 large eggs

Sauce

1 cup sugar
¼ cup water
½ cup butter
1 teaspoon vanilla extract

For the cake

1 Preheat oven to 350 F. Grease and flour a 10-inch Bundt pan.
2 In a large bowl, whisk together flour, baking powder, baking soda and salt.
3 In a small bowl, stir together vanilla and buttermilk.
4 In the bowl of an electric mixer on medium speed, cream butter and sugar for 5 minutes. Beat in eggs one at a time.
5 Add flour mixture to butter mixture, alternating with buttermilk mixture, beginning and ending with flour mixture.
6 Pour batter into Bundt pan and bake for 60 minutes.

For the sauce

1 Five minutes before you are going to take cake out of oven, make sauce: In a small saucepan over medium heat, bring sugar, water and butter to a low boil, stirring to dissolve sugar. Remove from heat and stir in vanilla.
2 Remove cake from oven and poke holes in top. Pour butter mixture over top and let it drip into holes. Let cake cool for about 10 minutes and then remove from pan promptly to prevent sticking.

Pairs Perfectly With a Cup of Coffee

Kentucky
Butter Cake

Cookies & Bars

THE ONLY PROBLEM WITH THESE RECIPES: THEY SMELL SO GOOD, THEY'RE GOING TO CAUSE A RUN ON YOUR KITCHEN BEFORE YOU EVEN TAKE THEM OUT OF THE OVEN... AND THEY TASTE EVEN BETTER!

Cranberry Drop
Cookies,
p. 80

TIP
This frosting
is worth the
10 minutes of
prep time!

Frosted Fudge Brownies

All-American • Company-Worthy • Easy

Rich chocolate frosting makes these brownies even
more irresistible.

PREP *15 minutes*

TOTAL *45 minutes*

YIELD *2 dozen*

Brownies

  1 cup plus 3 tablespoons butter, cubed
  ¾ cup cocoa powder
  4 eggs
  2 cups sugar
  1 teaspoon vanilla extract
1½ cups all-purpose flour
  1 teaspoon baking powder
  1 teaspoon salt

Frosting

  6 tablespoons butter, softened
2⅔ cups powdered sugar
  ½ cup cocoa
  1 teaspoon vanilla extract
  ⅓ cup milk

For the brownies

1 Preheat oven to 350 F. Coat a 13x9-inch baking pan with
cooking spray.

2 In a saucepan on low heat, melt butter. Remove from heat.
Stir in cocoa and let cool.

3 In the bowl of an electric mixer on medium speed, beat
eggs and sugar. Stir in vanilla and cooled butter mixture
until blended. Slowly whisk in flour, baking powder and salt.

4 Spread into prepared pan. Bake for 25 to 28 minutes.

5 Cool completely on wire rack before frosting.

For the frosting

1 In a large bowl, using a hand mixer on medium speed,
cream butter and powdered sugar until fluffy, 5 to 7 minutes.

2 Beat in cocoa and vanilla. Add enough milk for frosting
to achieve spreading consistency.

3 Spread onto brownies. Cut into bars.

TIP
You can use a white or yellow cake mix—the difference comes from egg yolks.

Gooey Butter Bars

Easy • Family Favorite

A boxed cake mix makes these quick to whip up—but your family will think you slaved in the kitchen for hours to make these delicious treats!

PREP *15 minutes*

TOTAL *45 minutes*

YIELD *18 bars*

Ingredients

- 1 (15.25-ounce) box white or yellow cake mix
- ½ cup butter, softened
- 1 egg
- 1 (8-ounce) package cream cheese, softened
- 2 eggs
- 4 cups powdered sugar

Instructions

1 Preheat oven to 350 F. Coat a 15x10x1-inch baking pan with cooking spray.

2 In the bowl of an electric mixer on low speed, combine cake mix, butter and egg until mixture is crumbly. Pat into bottom of pan and set aside.

3 In the same bowl, with mixer on medium, combine cream cheese and eggs and beat until mixture is smooth.

4 On low speed, add powdered sugar and beat until combined. Spread on top of crust.

5 Bake for 25 to 30 minutes or until filling is set and golden brown.

6 Cool in pan on wire rack, then cut into bars.

Soft and Filled With Flavor

Chewy Molasses Cookies

All-American • Easy • Holiday Classic

These soft, chewy cookies will soon become a household favorite.

PREP *30 minutes*

TOTAL *45 minutes; 1 hour inactive*

YIELD *2 dozen*

Cookies

- ¾ cup butter, softened
- 1 cup brown sugar
- ⅓ cup molasses
- 1 egg
- 2½ cups all-purpose flour
- 2 teaspoons baking soda
- 2 teaspoons pumpkin pie spice
- ½ teaspoon salt

Icing

- 1½ cups powdered sugar
- ½ teaspoon vanilla extract
- 3 tablespoons milk

For the cookies

1 In the bowl of an electric mixer on medium speed, cream butter and brown sugar until fluffy, about 1 minute.

2 Add molasses, then beat in egg.

3 On low speed, gradually add flour, baking soda, pumpkin pie spice and salt. Cover and chill dough for 1 hour.

4 Preheat oven to 325 F. Line a baking sheet with parchment paper.

5 Roll dough into 1-inch balls and place on prepared baking sheet, spaced 2 inches apart. Flatten balls slightly.

6 Bake for 12 to 14 minutes.

7 Cool on cookie sheet for 10 minutes, then remove to wire rack and cool completely.

For the icing

1 In a medium bowl, stir together powdered sugar, vanilla and milk.

2 Spoon icing on top of each cookie and spread with back of spoon.

*TIP
Sub potato chips, breakfast cereal or even bacon bits for the pretzels.*

Butterscotch Pretzel Cookies

All-American • Easy • Family Favorite

Sound crazy to add pretzels to cookie dough? Try it...the salty crunch is addictive!

PREP *15 minutes*

TOTAL *30 minutes; 30 minutes inactive*

YIELD *3 dozen*

Ingredients

- 1 cup butter, softened
- 1 cup sugar
- 1 cup brown sugar
- 2 eggs
- 1 teaspoon vanilla extract
- 2½ cups all-purpose flour
- 1 tablespoon cornstarch
- ½ teaspoon salt
- 1 teaspoon baking soda
- 2½ cups butterscotch chips, divided
- 2 cups crushed pretzels

Instructions

1 Line 2 baking sheets with parchment paper.

2 In the bowl of an electric mixer on medium speed, cream butter and both sugars.

3 Add eggs one at a time, then stir in vanilla. On low speed, beat in flour, cornstarch, salt and baking soda.

4 Fold in 2 cups of butterscotch chips and pretzels.

5 Form 2 tablespoons of dough into balls and place on prepared baking sheets. Press remaining ½ cup butterscotch chips into top of cookies.

6 Refrigerate balls for at least 30 minutes.

7 Preheat oven to 350 F. Bake for about 13 to 15 minutes, or until golden brown.

8 Cool on baking sheets for 5 minutes, then remove to wire racks to cool completely.

Turtle Cookies

Company-Worthy • Easy • Family Favorite

Love turtle candies? Just wait until you try the cookie version!

PREP *15 minutes*

TOTAL *25 minutes*

YIELD *3 dozen*

Ingredients

- 1 cup butter, softened
- ¾ cup sugar
- ¾ cup brown sugar
- 2 eggs
- 2 teaspoons vanilla extract
- 2¼ cups all-purpose flour
- 1 teaspoon baking soda
- ½ teaspoon salt
- ¾ cup chopped pecans
- 1 (12-ounce) bag semisweet chocolate chips
- ¾ cup caramel bits

Instructions

1 Preheat oven to 375 F. Line 2 baking sheets with parchment paper.

2 In the bowl of an electric mixer on medium speed, cream butter with sugars until fluffy.

3 Beat in eggs, one at a time. Add vanilla.

4 On low speed, gradually add flour, baking soda and salt. Fold in pecans, chocolate chips and caramel bits.

5 Drop tablespoons of dough onto prepared baking sheets.

6 Bake for 9 to 11 minutes or until lightly browned.

7 Cool on baking sheet for 3 minutes, then remove to wire racks to cool completely.

Turtle
Cookies

You'll Want to Make a Double Batch!

Give Sugar Cookies an Upgrade

Frosted Pumpkin Sugar Cookies

All-American • Easy • Family Favorite

Can't get enough pumpkin spice? These cookies are full of everyone's favorite fall flavor.

PREP *20 minutes*

TOTAL *30 minutes*

YIELD *3 dozen*

Cookies

- ½ cup butter, softened
- ½ cup vegetable oil
- ½ cup pumpkin puree
- 1 cup sugar
- ½ cup powdered sugar
- ½ teaspoon vanilla extract
- 2 eggs
- 4 cups all-purpose flour
- 1 teaspoon pumpkin pie spice
- ¼ teaspoon baking soda
- ¼ teaspoon cream of tartar
- ½ teaspoon salt

Frosting

- 2 cups powdered sugar
- 3 tablespoons milk
- ¼ teaspoon pumpkin pie spice

For the cookies

1 Preheat oven to 350 F. Line 2 baking sheets with parchment paper.

2 In the bowl of an electric mixer on medium speed, beat butter, oil, pumpkin puree, sugars, vanilla and eggs until smooth.

3 Gradually add flour, pumpkin pie spice, baking soda, cream of tartar and salt and blend until incorporated.

4 Roll 2 tablespoons of dough into a ball and place on prepared baking sheets.

5 Use bottom of a glass to press down on each dough ball to flatten.

6 Bake cookies for 8 to 9 minutes.

For the frosting

1 While cookies bake, in a medium bowl, whisk together powdered sugar, milk and pumpkin pie spice.

2 Cool cookies on baking sheet for 2 minutes before frosting. (Cookies should still be warm when you frost them.)

3 Spread frosting onto each cookie and let sit for several minutes to give them time to firm up.

Chocolate Chip Skillet Slices

All-American • Easy • Family Favorite

Baking chocolate chip cookies in a cast-iron skillet keeps all the rich, yummy flavors together.

PREP *10 minutes*

TOTAL *35 minutes*

YIELD *8 servings*

Ingredients

- ½ cup butter, softened
- ½ cup brown sugar
- 1 teaspoon vanilla extract
- 1 egg
- 1½ cups all-purpose flour
- ½ teaspoon baking soda
- ½ teaspoon salt
- ¾ cup semisweet chocolate morsels

Instructions

1 Preheat oven to 350 F. Lightly grease a 10-inch cast-iron skillet.

2 In the bowl of an electric mixer on medium speed, cream butter and sugar until fluffy.

3 Beat in vanilla and egg. On low speed, gradually beat in flour, baking soda and salt.

4 Fold in chocolate morsels, then spread batter into prepared skillet.

5 Bake for 20 to 25 minutes. Remove from oven and cool, then slice into wedges.

**Pie-Shaped
Cookies?
Yes, Please!**

Frosted Maple
Cookies

Frosted Maple Cookies

All-American • Family Favorite

Introduce this classic cookie back to your kitchen to enjoy today!

PREP *35 minutes*

TOTAL *45 minutes; 1 hour inactive*

YIELD *3 dozen*

Cookies

- ½ cup butter, softened
- 1½ cups brown sugar
- 2 eggs
- 1 cup sour cream
- 1 tablespoon maple syrup
- 2¾ cups all-purpose flour
- 1 teaspoon salt
- ½ teaspoon baking soda

Frosting

- ½ cup butter, softened
- 2 cups powdered sugar
- 1 teaspoon maple syrup
- 3 tablespoons hot water

For the cookies

1 Preheat oven to 375 F. Coat baking sheets with cooking spray.

2 In the bowl of an electric mixer on medium speed, cream together butter and sugar for 5 minutes. Add eggs, one at a time, beating well after each one. Stir in sour cream and maple syrup.

3 On low speed, gradually add flour, salt and baking soda and mix until incorporated. Cover and refrigerate for 1 hour.

4 Drop tablespoonfuls of dough onto prepared baking sheet, spacing them 2 inches apart.

5 Bake for 8 to 10 minutes or until edges are lightly browned. Cool completely on wire racks.

For the frosting

1 In a small saucepan over low heat, melt butter and cook until golden brown.

2 Remove from heat; stir in powdered sugar, maple syrup and water until it has a spreadable consistency.

3 Frost cooled cookies.

TIP
Save this recipe for the annual holiday cookie exchange!

Fruitcake Cookies

Company-Worthy • Easy

Packed with dried fruit and pecans, these chewy, two-bite nibbles bring out the festive spirit.

PREP *20 minutes*

TOTAL *40 minutes*

YIELD *3 dozen*

Ingredients

- ¾ cup sugar
- ½ cup butter, softened
- 2 eggs
- ½ teaspoon vanilla extract
- 1½ cups all-purpose flour
- ½ teaspoon baking soda
- ½ teaspoon salt
- ½ pound mixed candied fruit and peel
- 2 cups chopped toasted pecans
- ½ cup golden raisins
- ½ cup maraschino cherries, chopped

Instructions

1 Preheat oven to 300 F. Line 2 baking sheets with parchment paper.

2 In the bowl of an electric mixer on medium speed, cream sugar and butter until fluffy. Beat in eggs, one at a time, then stir in vanilla.

3 At low speed, gradually add flour, baking soda and salt and mix until thoroughly incorporated.

4 Fold in candied fruit and peel, pecans, raisins and cherries.

5 Drop dough by spoonfuls onto prepared baking sheets, spacing them 1 inch apart. Bake 18 to 20 minutes.

6 Let cool on baking sheets for 2 minutes, then remove to wire racks to cool completely.

Cherry Nut Cookies

All-American • Easy • Holiday Classic

Feel free to substitute raisins or dried cranberries for the dried cherries.

PREP *15 minutes*

TOTAL *25 minutes*

YIELD *2 dozen*

Ingredients

- ¾ cup butter
- ¾ cup sugar
- ¾ cup firmly packed brown sugar
- 2 large eggs
- 1 teaspoon vanilla extract
- 1½ cups all-purpose flour
- 1 teaspoon baking soda
- 1 teaspoon ground cinnamon
- ½ teaspoon salt
- 2¾ cups old-fashioned rolled oats
- 1 cup dried cherries
- 1 cup chopped walnuts

Instructions

1 Preheat oven to 350 F. Coat baking sheets with cooking spray.

2 In the bowl of an electric mixer on medium speed, cream butter and both sugars until fluffy. Beat in eggs and vanilla.

3 On low speed, add flour, baking soda, cinnamon and salt and mix until well incorporated. Fold in oats, cherries and walnuts.

4 Drop dough by tablespoonfuls onto prepared baking sheets. Bake for 9 to 11 minutes or until lightly browned.

5 Cool cookies 2 minutes on baking sheets, then remove to wire rack to cool completely.

Oatmeal
Raisin Gets
a Makeover

Twice the Chocolaty Goodness

TIP
For more fudgy brownies, take them out of the oven a little early.

Double Chocolate Brownies

All-American • Easy • Family Favorite

Chocolate fans rejoice! There's even more to love in this rich and delicious brownie recipe.

PREP *15 minutes*

TOTAL *35 minutes*

YIELD *24 servings*

Ingredients

- ½ cup butter
- 1 (12-ounce package) semisweet chocolate chips, divided
- 3 eggs
- 1 teaspoon vanilla extract
- 1¼ cups all-purpose flour
- 1 cup sugar
- ¼ teaspoon baking soda

Instructions

1 Preheat oven to 350 F. Coat a 13x9-inch baking pan with cooking spray.

2 In a heavy-duty saucepan over low heat, melt butter and 1 cup chocolate chips; stir until smooth. Let cool 2 minutes, then stir in eggs and vanilla.

3 Beat in flour, sugar and baking soda.

4 Fold in remaining chocolate chips and spread batter into prepared baking pan.

5 Bake for 18 to 22 minutes.

6 Cool completely in pan on wire rack.

7 Cut into bars.

Double Chocolate Maple Bars

All-American • Easy • Family Favorite

The frosting on these chocolate maple bars is simply outstanding!

PREP *20 minutes*

TOTAL *1 hour*

YIELD *12 bars*

Bars

- ½ cup butter
- ¾ cup maple syrup
- ½ cup sugar
- 3 eggs
- 3 tablespoons milk
- 1 teaspoon vanilla extract
- 1¼ cups all-purpose flour
- ¼ teaspoon baking powder
- ¼ teaspoon salt
- 1½ squares (1½ ounces) unsweetened chocolate, melted
- ½ cup chopped walnuts
- ½ cup flaked coconut

Frosting

- ¼ cup butter, softened
- 1 cup powdered sugar
- ½ cup unsweetened cocoa powder
- ½ cup pure maple syrup

For the bars

1 Preheat oven to 350 F. Grease a 13x9-inch baking pan.

2 In the bowl of an electric mixer on medium speed, cream butter, syrup and sugar until fluffy. Beat in eggs one by one. Stir in milk and vanilla.

3 On low speed, slowly beat in flour, baking powder and salt.

4 Remove half of batter to another bowl.

5 In a small bowl, combine melted chocolate and walnuts; add to one half of batter, and then spread into prepared baking pan.

6 Add coconut to remaining batter. Spread over chocolate-walnut batter.

7 Bake for 20 to 25 minutes, or until a toothpick inserted in center comes out clean. Cool completely on a wire rack.

For the frosting

1 In the bowl of a standing mixer, cream butter, powdered sugar and cocoa.

2 Slowly add syrup, beating until smooth and spreadable. Frost bars.

TIP
Milk and dark chocolate chips are also delicious in this recipe.

White Chocolate Macadamia Cookies

All-American • Company-Worthy • Easy

These will be the star of any cookie exchange. You can use walnuts instead of macadamias, if you'd prefer.

PREP *15 minutes*

TOTAL *30 minutes*

YIELD *15 cookies*

Ingredients

- ½ cup butter, softened
- ½ cup brown sugar
- ¼ cup sugar
- 1 egg
- ½ teaspoon vanilla extract
- 1½ cups all-purpose flour
- 1 teaspoon baking soda
- ½ teaspoon salt
- ¾ cup chopped macadamia nuts
- ¾ cup white chocolate chips

Instructions

1 Preheat oven to 350 F. Line a baking sheet with parchment paper.

2 In the bowl of an electric mixer on medium speed, cream butter and sugars until fluffy. Add egg and vanilla and beat well.

3 Slowly add flour, baking soda and salt, beating until just incorporated. Fold in nuts and white chocolate chips.

4 Drop 2 tablespoonfuls of dough onto baking sheets, spacing them 2 inches apart.

5 Bake for 10 to 13 minutes, until edges are golden brown and centers are slightly underdone.

6 Let cool completely on baking sheets on wire racks.

*White
Chocolate
Macadamia
Cookies*

Oatmeal
Raisin
Cookies

Vanilla Walnut Fudge

Oatmeal Raisin Cookies

All-American • Easy • Family Favorite

Do not overbake these cookies! The edges should be just lightly browned.

PREP *20 minutes*

TOTAL *1 hour*

YIELD *2 dozen*

Ingredients

- 1 cup butter, softened
- 1 cup brown sugar
- ½ cup sugar
- 2 eggs
- 1 teaspoon vanilla extract
- 1½ cups all-purpose flour
- 1 teaspoon baking soda
- 1 teaspoon ground cinnamon
- 1½ cups raisins
- 3 cups old-fashioned oats

Instructions

1 Preheat oven to 350 F. Coat two large baking sheets with cooking spray.

2 In the bowl of an electric mixer on medium speed, cream butter and both sugars until fluffy, about 3 minutes. Beat in eggs, one at a time. Add vanilla.

3 Stir in flour, baking soda and cinnamon. Fold in raisins and oats.

4 Drop dough by rounded tablespoonfuls onto prepared baking sheets, spacing them 2 inches apart.

5 Bake for 10 to 12 minutes. (Note: The cookies will seem underdone.)

6 Cool 1 minute on baking sheets. Remove to a wire rack and cool completely.

Vanilla Walnut Fudge

Easy • Family Favorite

You don't need a candy thermometer on hand to make this delicious fudge.

PREP *5 minutes*

TOTAL *4 hours 5 minutes*

YIELD *36 servings (1-inch pieces)*

Ingredients

- 2 (12-ounce) bars white chocolate, chopped
- 1 (14-ounce) can sweetened condensed milk
- ¼ cup butter
- 1 teaspoon vanilla extract
- 1½ cups chopped, toasted walnuts

Instructions

1 Grease an 8-inch square baking pan.

2 In a medium glass bowl, combine white chocolate, condensed milk and butter. Heat in microwave for 1 to 2 minutes.

3 Stir to combine. Heat another 15 seconds. Stir and heat an additional 15 seconds, stirring until smooth.

4 Add vanilla and walnuts, stirring to combine. Pour into prepared pan.

5 Chill until ready to serve, about 4 hours.

6 Slice into 1-inch squares and store in an airtight container in refrigerator.

A Cookie Jar Favorite!

TIP
Giving cookies as a gift? Stack them in a wide-mouth mason jar or a decorative mailing tube.

Snickerdoodles

All-American • Easy • Family Favorite

Since you don't have to chill the dough, these can be made in a hurry.

PREP *10 minutes*

TOTAL *20 minutes*

YIELD *20 cookies*

Ingredients

- 1 cup butter, softened
- 1 cup granulated sugar, divided
- ½ cup light brown sugar
- 1 egg
- 1 egg yolk
- 2 teaspoons vanilla extract
- 2¾ cups all-purpose flour
- 1 teaspoon baking soda
- 1 teaspoon cream of tartar
- ½ teaspoon salt
- 4 teaspoons ground cinnamon, divided

Instructions

1 Preheat oven to 325 F. Line a baking sheet with parchment paper.

2 In the bowl of an electric mixer on medium speed, cream butter, ¾ cup granulated sugar and brown sugar until fluffy.

3 Add egg, egg yolk and vanilla, and beat for 1 minute.

4 On low speed, add flour, baking soda, cream of tartar, salt and 1 teaspoon cinnamon, mixing until just combined.

5 In a small bowl, stir together remaining cinnamon and remaining sugar, stirring until evenly combined.

6 Form 2 tablespoonfuls of dough into balls, then roll each ball in cinnamon-sugar mixture.

7 Place balls on prepared baking sheet, spacing them 2 inches apart. Bake for 10 to 12 minutes.

8 Let cool on baking sheets for 2 minutes, then remove to wire racks to cool completely.

Cranberry Drop Cookies

All-American • Easy • Holiday Classic

Whip up these drop cookies where cranberries get star billing. You can also try stirring in a half cup of nuts.

PREP *15 minutes*

TOTAL *30 minutes*

YIELD *4 dozen*

Ingredients

- ½ cup butter, softened
- 1 cup sugar
- 1 cup brown sugar
- 1 egg
- ¼ cup milk
- 2 tablespoons lemon juice
- 3 cups all-purpose flour
- 1 teaspoon baking powder
- ¼ teaspoon baking soda
- ½ teaspoon salt
- 1 cup dried cranberries

Instructions

1 Preheat oven to 375 F. Line baking sheets with parchment paper.

2 In the bowl of an electric mixer on medium speed, cream butter and sugars until fluffy.

3 Beat in egg, milk and lemon juice.

4 At low speed, add flour, baking powder, baking soda and salt and blend until incorporated. Fold in cranberries.

5 Drop dough by heaping teaspoons onto prepared baking sheets.

6 Bake for 12 to 15 minutes or until golden brown.

Chocolate Chip Biscotti

Easy • Family Favorite

These crisp cookies are perfect for dunking into hot chocolate or coffee.

PREP *20 minutes*

TOTAL *1 hour, 5 minutes*

YIELD *30 servings*

Ingredients

- ½ cup butter, softened
- 1 cup sugar
- 2 eggs
- 2 teaspoons vanilla extract
- 2 cups all-purpose flour
- ¼ cup cocoa powder
- 1 teaspoon baking soda
- 1 teaspoon salt
- 1 cup semisweet chocolate morsels

Instructions

1 Preheat oven to 350 F. Line a baking sheet with parchment paper.

2 In the bowl of an electric mixer on medium speed, cream butter and sugar for 2 minutes or until fluffy.

3 Add eggs, one at a time, then beat in vanilla.

4 On low speed, gradually beat in flour, cocoa powder, baking soda and salt. Fold in chocolate chips.

5 Shape dough into a ball, then divide it in two.

6 Place both pieces on prepared baking sheet. Form each into a log about 7 inches long and 2 inches wide.

7 Bake for 35 minutes or until firm to the touch. Let cool for 5 minutes; keep oven on.

8 Transfer logs to a wooden cutting board. Using a sharp knife, cut logs into ¾-inch slices. Place slices, cut side down, back on baking sheet and bake for 10 more minutes.

9 Cool on baking sheet for 5 minutes, then transfer to a wire rack to cool completely.

Cranberry
Drop Cookies

TIP
Biscotti will keep up to three months in the freezer in an airtight container.

Chocolate Chip Biscotti

Pumpkin Spice Whoopie Pies

All-American • Family Favorite

Fridge-chilled whoopie pies are easier to eat because the filling doesn't squish out of the sides.

PREP *40 minutes*

TOTAL *1 hour; 30 minutes inactive*

YIELD *3 dozen*

Cookies

1	cup vegetable oil
2	cups brown sugar
2	eggs
1½	cups pumpkin puree
1	teaspoon vanilla extract
3	cups all-purpose flour
1	teaspoon salt
1	teaspoon baking powder
1	teaspoon baking soda
2	tablespoons pumpkin pie spice

Filling

4	tablespoons milk
1	teaspoon vanilla extract
2¼	cups powdered sugar, divided
¾	cup shortening, softened

For the cookies

1 Preheat oven to 350 F. Line 2 baking sheets with parchment paper.

2 In the bowl of an electric mixer on medium speed, beat oil and brown sugar until combined.

3 Add in eggs, one at a time, then pumpkin puree and vanilla; blend until incorporated.

4 On low speed, gradually add flour, salt, baking powder, baking soda and pumpkin pie spice until incorporated.

5 Drop dough by tablespoonfuls onto prepared baking sheets.

6 Bake for 10 to 12 minutes. Let cool on baking sheets.

For the filling

1 In a medium bowl, whisk together milk, vanilla and 1 cup powdered sugar.

2 Beat in shortening and remaining powdered sugar until fluffy.

3 Spread filling between two cookies to make pies.

4 Refrigerate until chilled.

TIP
You can use foil to line baking sheets instead of parchment paper.

Coconut Pecan Cookies

Easy • Family Favorite

These mouthwatering treats are a cross between pecan sandies and snickerdoodles.

PREP *15 minutes*

TOTAL *25 minutes*

YIELD *4 dozen*

Ingredients

1	cup butter, softened
1	cup brown sugar
1¼	cups granulated sugar, divided
2	eggs
1	teaspoon vanilla extract
2½	cups all-purpose flour
1	teaspoon baking soda
1	cup shredded coconut
1	cup chopped pecans
1	teaspoon cinnamon

Instructions

1 Preheat over to 350 F. Line baking sheets with parchment paper.

2 In the bowl of an electric mixer on medium speed, cream butter, brown sugar and 1 cup granulated sugar until fluffy. Beat in eggs one at a time, then stir in vanilla.

3 On low speed, gradually add flour and baking soda, then fold in coconut and pecans.

4 In a small bowl, stir together remaining sugar and cinnamon.

5 Form dough into 1-inch balls, then roll in cinnamon sugar and place on prepared baking sheet.

6 Bake for 10 to 12 minutes or until browned.

7 Cool on baking sheet for 2 minutes and then transfer to wire rack to cool completely.

For Coconut Fans

Coconut
Pecan
Cookies

Quick Breads & Muffins

THESE SWEET TREATS ARE A WONDERFUL WAY TO START THE MORNING OR MAKE AN AFTERNOON BREAK MEMORABLE. PLUS, THEY CAN BE WHIPPED UP IN JUST MINUTES.

Chocolate Chip Pumpkin Bread,
p. 99

Double Nut Muffins

Easy • Family Favorite

Pecan-pie lovers won't be able to get enough of these.

PREP *10 minutes*

TOTAL *25 minutes; 10 minutes inactive*

YIELD *12 muffins*

Ingredients

- 1 cup butter, softened
- 2 eggs, beaten
- 1½ cups light brown sugar
- 1 cup flour
- 1 cup chopped pecans
- 1 cup chopped walnuts

Instructions

1 Preheat oven to 350 F. Line a muffin pan with 12 paper liners and set aside.

2 In a large bowl, whisk butter and eggs until smooth. Beat in brown sugar and flour, then fold in pecans and walnuts just until combined.

3 Spoon mixture into prepared muffin tin. Bake for 15 to 17 minutes.

4 Cool on wire rack for 10 minutes.

*Cranberry
Banana Bread*

TIP
Very ripe
bananas make
the most
flavorful
bread.

Cranberry Banana Bread

All-American • Easy • Family Favorite

Tangy cranberries take this bread to the next level!

PREP *15 minutes*

TOTAL *1 hour 25 minutes*

YIELD *8 servings*

Bread

- 1 cup sugar
- ½ cup butter, softened
- 2 eggs
- ¼ cup milk
- 1 teaspoon vanilla extract
- 2 cups flour
- 2 teaspoons baking powder
- 3 bananas, mashed
- ½ cup walnuts
- 1 cup dried cranberries

Glaze

- 2 cups powdered sugar
- 4 tablespoons milk
- 1 teaspoon vanilla extract

For the bread

1 Preheat oven to 350 F. Grease an 8x4-inch loaf pan.

2 In a medium bowl, using a hand mixer, cream sugar and butter.

3 Beat in eggs, then add milk and vanilla. Gradually beat in flour and baking powder.

4 Gently stir in bananas. Fold in walnuts and cranberries.

5 Spread mixture into prepared pan.

6 Bake 1 hour and 10 minutes or until a toothpick inserted in center comes out clean.

7 Cool 10 minutes on rack; remove from pan.

For the glaze

In a bowl, whisk all ingredients together; drizzle over bread.

Carrot Coconut Bread

All-American • Easy • Family Favorite

Sour cream makes this loaf extra moist.

PREP *30 minutes*

TOTAL *1 hour, 30 minutes*

YIELD *10 servings*

Bread

- ½ cup vegetable oil
- ½ cup brown sugar
- ¼ cup sugar
- 2 eggs
- 1 teaspoon coconut extract
- ½ cup sour cream
- 1 teaspoon cinnamon
- ½ teaspoon nutmeg
- ½ teaspoon ground cloves
- ½ teaspoon salt
- 1 teaspoon baking powder
- ½ teaspoon baking soda
- 1½ cups flour
- 1¼ cups shredded carrots
- 1 cup sweetened coconut flakes

Frosting

- 2 ounces cream cheese, softened
- 1 cup powdered sugar
- 1 tablespoon milk
- ¼ cup toasted coconut

For the bread

1 Preheat oven to 350 F. Coat an 8x5-inch loaf pan with cooking spray.

2 In a large bowl, using an electric hand mixer, beat oil and both sugars until fluffy.

3 Whisk in eggs, coconut extract and sour cream and beat until blended.

4 Slowly add cinnamon, nutmeg, cloves, salt, baking powder, baking soda and flour until blended. Fold in carrots and coconut.

5 Spoon into prepared loaf pan and bake for 60 minutes or until a toothpick comes out clean. (Cover with foil if bread starts to brown too much in the last 10 minutes of baking.)

6 Remove from oven and cool in pan for 15 minutes. Remove from pan and place on a wire rack to cool completely.

For the frosting

1 In a medium bowl,using a hand mixer, beat cream cheese and powdered sugar until fluffy. Stir in milk until it has a spreadable consistency.

2 Frost bread and top with toasted coconut right away so it sticks. Store, covered, in refrigerator.

Mini Orange Cranberry Scones With Apple Butter

Easy • Family Favorite

Slightly tart fruit tempers the sweetness of these little pastries.

PREP *25 minutes*

TOTAL *40 minutes; 10 minutes inactive*

YIELD *18 scones*

Ingredients

1	teaspoon orange zest
1¼	cups all-purpose flour
¼	cup powdered sugar
2	teaspoons baking powder
½	teaspoon salt
⅓	cup dried cranberries
1	cup heavy cream
	Apple butter

Instructions

1 Preheat oven to 400 F. Line a baking sheet with parchment paper.

2 In a large bowl, stir together zest, flour, sugar, baking powder, salt and cranberries.

3 Stir in cream until a dough forms.

4 Place dough on a surface dusted generously with flour. Divide it into 3 pieces.

5 Shape each piece into a 3-inch disc.

6 Cut each disc into 6 wedges.

7 Place on prepared baking sheet. Bake for 15 minutes.

8 Cool on wire rack for 10 minutes before serving. Serve with apple butter, if desired.

Apple Pie Loaf Bread

All-American • Easy • Family Favorite

A swivel-blade peeler will make quick work of the skin on your apples.

PREP *15 minutes*

TOTAL *1 hour 15 minutes; 1 hour 10 minutes inactive*

YIELD *12 servings*

Ingredients

⅔	cup sugar
½	cup sour cream
2	eggs
⅔	cup applesauce
1	teaspoon vanilla extract
7	tablespoons butter, melted, divided
1¾	cups plus 1 tablespoon flour, divided
1	teaspoon baking soda
1	teaspoon apple pie spice
½	teaspoon salt
1	cup peeled, chopped apples
½	cup chopped walnuts
¼	cup brown sugar
½	teaspoon cinnamon

Instructions

1 Preheat oven to 350 F. Grease a 9x5-inch loaf pan.

2 In a large bowl, using a hand mixer, beat sugar, sour cream and eggs until well combined.

3 Stir in applesauce, vanilla and 6 tablespoons melted butter until just incorporated.

4 In a medium bowl, whisk together 1¾ cups flour, baking soda, apple pie spice and salt.

5 Add flour mixture to egg mixture. Fold in apples and spoon into prepared pan.

6 Stir together walnuts, remaining 1 tablespoon melted butter, remaining 1 tablespoon flour, brown sugar and cinnamon. Sprinkle evenly over batter.

7 Bake for 55 to 60 minutes or until a toothpick inserted in center comes out clean.

8 Cool in pan for 10 minutes. Remove from pan and cool completely on wire rack, about 1 hour.

Mini Orange Cranberry Scones With Apple Butter

Apple Pie
Loaf Bread

S'mores Bread

All-American • Family Favorite

Now you can enjoy your favorite childhood campfire treat year-round—no firepit necessary!

PREP *25 minutes*

TOTAL *1 hour 15 minutes; 1 hour inactive*

YIELD *12 servings*

Ingredients

- ½ cup graham cracker crumbs
- 1 cup all-purpose flour
- ½ cup unsweetened cocoa powder
- ½ teaspoon salt
- 1 teaspoon baking powder
- ¼ teaspoon baking soda
- 1 cup vegetable oil
- 1 cup brown sugar
- 2 eggs
- 1 teaspoon vanilla extract
- ⅔ cup sour cream
- ¾ cup chocolate chips
- 4 rectangular graham crackers, broken into quarters
- 1½ cups mini marshmallows, divided
  Graham crackers and squares of chocolate bar, for decorating

Instructions

1 Preheat oven to 350 F. Grease a 9x5-inch loaf pan.

2 In a medium bowl, stir together graham cracker crumbs, flour, cocoa, salt, baking powder and baking soda.

3 In a large bowl, beat together oil, brown sugar, eggs, vanilla and sour cream. Stir in graham cracker mixture until combined.

4 Fold in chocolate chips, quartered graham crackers and ¾ cup of mini marshmallows.

5 Pour batter into prepared pan and bake for 50 to 60 minutes, or until a knife inserted into center of bread comes out with moist crumbs.

6 Let bread cool in pan for 10 minutes, then remove to a rack to cool completely, about 1 hour.

7 Turn on broiler. Top bread with remaining ¾ cup of mini marshmallows and broil.

8 Decorate with graham crackers and chocolate squares, if desired.

TIP
No muffin tin? Use foil cupcake liners, which hold their shape on their own.

Chocolate Chip Coffee Muffins

All-American • Easy • Family Favorite

Instant-coffee powder enhances the richness of chocolate without adding more liquid to the recipe.

PREP *15 minutes*

TOTAL *35 minutes; 15 minutes inactive*

YIELD *12 muffins*

Ingredients

- 1 egg
- 1 cup milk
- ¼ cup butter, melted
- 1 teaspoon vanilla extract
- 2 cups all-purpose flour
- ¾ cup sugar
- 2 teaspoons baking powder
- 2 teaspoons instant-coffee powder
- ½ teaspoon salt
- 1 cup semisweet chocolate chips

Instructions

1 Preheat oven to 375 F. Line a muffin pan with 12 paper liners and set aside.

2 In a large bowl, whisk together egg, milk, butter and vanilla.

3 Stir in flour, sugar, baking powder, instant coffee and salt just until combined. Fold in chocolate chips.

4 Spoon into prepared muffin pan.

5 Bake for 15 to 20 minutes. Let cool in pan for 15 minutes on wire rack.

Chocolate for Breakfast... Why Not?

Chocolate
Chip Coffee
Muffins

Our Favorite Way to Eat Veggies!

Zucchini
Bread

Zucchini Bread

All-American • Easy • Family Favorite

Small zucchini are sweeter, and therefore better for baking.

PREP *15 minutes*

TOTAL *1 hour 15 minutes; 1 hour inactive*

YIELD *16 servings*

Ingredients

  3 eggs
  1 cup canola oil
  2 cups sugar
  1 teaspoon vanilla extract
  3 cups all-purpose flour
  1 teaspoon baking soda
  1 teaspoon baking powder
  1 tablespoon cinnamon
  ½ teaspoon salt
  2 cups grated zucchini
  ½ cup chopped walnuts

Instructions

1 Preheat oven to 325 F. Grease two 9x5-inch loaf pans.

2 Combine all ingredients except zucchini and walnuts in a large bowl. Mix until just combined. Fold in zucchini.

3 Divide batter evenly between two loaf pans and sprinkle walnuts on top.

4 Bake for 1 hour or until a toothpick inserted in center comes out clean.

5 Cool on a wire rack for 1 hour before slicing.

Strawberry Walnut Quick Bread

Easy • Family Favorite

Stock up on strawberries during the summer and freeze them so that you always have a supply to make this yummy bread.

PREP *20 minutes*

TOTAL *1 hour 10 minutes*

YIELD *10 servings*

Bread

  2 cups strawberries, chopped in ½-inch pieces
  ¾ cup sugar, divided
  1½ cups all-purpose flour
  ¼ teaspoon ground nutmeg
  ¼ teaspoon ground cinnamon
  ½ teaspoon salt
  1 teaspoon baking soda
  1 egg, beaten
  1 teaspoon vanilla extract
  ⅓ cup butter, melted
  1 cup chopped walnuts

Glaze

  1½ cups powdered sugar
  ½ teaspoon vanilla extract
  2 tablespoons milk
  ¼ cup finely diced fresh strawberries

For the bread

1 Preheat oven to 350 F. Coat a 9x5-inch loaf pan with cooking spray.

2 Place strawberries in a medium bowl. Sprinkle with 1 teaspoon of sugar and toss to combine.

3 In a separate bowl, combine flour, remaining sugar, nutmeg, cinnamon, salt and baking soda.

4 Make a well in flour mixture, and add egg, vanilla and butter. Gradually stir into flour mixture. Fold in strawberries and walnuts.

5 Spoon into loaf pan. Bake for 45 to 50 minutes or until a toothpick inserted in center comes out clean.

6 Cool on a wire rack.

For the glaze

1 Whisk together powdered sugar, vanilla and milk in a medium bowl until smooth. Fold in strawberries.

2 Drizzle over bread.

TIP
No buttermilk? Use a scant ¼ cup of milk and ¾ teaspoon of lemon juice or vinegar for ¼ cup buttermilk.

Apple Snack Bread

All-American • Easy • Family Favorite

Serve this delicious quick bread any time of the day. It's made in one bowl, so cleanup is a cinch!

PREP *15 minutes*

TOTAL *55 minutes; 1 hour inactive*

YIELD *9 servings*

Ingredients

- ½ cup canola oil
- ½ cup plus 2 tablespoons sugar, divided
- ½ cup brown sugar
- 1 teaspoon vanilla extract
- 2 eggs
- ¼ cup buttermilk
- 1¼ cups flour
- ¼ teaspoon salt
- 1 teaspoon baking powder
- ¼ teaspoon baking soda
- 2 Granny Smith apples, peeled, cored and cubed
- 1 teaspoon cinnamon

Instructions

1 Preheat oven to 350 F. Grease an 8-inch square pan and line with parchment paper.

2 In a large bowl whisk together oil, ½ cup sugar, brown sugar, vanilla, eggs and buttermilk.

3 Stir in flour, salt, baking powder and baking soda just until combined.

4 Pour batter into prepared pan.

5 In the same bowl, toss apples, cinnamon and remaining sugar.
Spoon over batter.

6 Bake for 35 to 40 minutes. Cool on wire rack for 1 hour before slicing.

Pecan Coffee Cake

All-American • Family Favorite

Pecans are popular in recipes because they develop a crunchy texture and rich flavor while in the oven. Yum!

PREP *20 minutes*

TOTAL *50 minutes*

YIELD *9 servings*

Ingredients

- 3 tablespoons butter, melted
- ⅔ cup light brown sugar
- 1 teaspoon cinnamon
- 2 tablespoons all-purpose flour
- 1½ cups finely chopped pecans
- ½ cup butter, softened
- 1 cup sugar
- 2 eggs
- 1 tablespoon vanilla extract
- 1 cup sour cream
- ½ teaspoon salt
- 1 teaspoon baking powder
- ¾ teaspoon baking soda
- 1¾ cups all-purpose flour

Instructions

1 Preheat oven to 350 F. Coat a 9x5-inch baking dish with cooking spray.

2 In a medium bowl, make streusel: Stir together butter, brown sugar, cinnamon, flour and pecans until combined. Set aside.

3 In the bowl of an electric mixer on medium speed, cream butter and sugar until fluffy, about 2 minutes.

4 Add eggs one at a time, and beat for 2 minutes. Stir in vanilla and sour cream until blended.

5 Add salt, baking powder and baking soda. Gradually add flour until just combined. Don't overmix.

6 Spread half of batter in bottom of prepared baking dish. Sprinkle half of streusel mixture on top of batter. Spread remaining batter on top of streusel and sprinkle remaining streusel on top.

7 Bake for 30 to 35 minutes. Cool on wire rack.

Worth Getting Out of Bed For!

Pecan Coffee Cake

*Gingerbread
Scones*

Perfect for
Afternoon Tea

Chocolate Chip Pumpkin Bread

TIP
A teaspoon of ground cinnamon and a ¼ teaspoon of nutmeg can sub for the pumpkin pie spice.

Gingerbread Scones

Easy • Family Favorite • Holiday Classic

These delicious scones taste best with a pat of butter on top.

PREP *25 minutes*

TOTAL *40 minutes*

YIELD *8 servings*

Ingredients

- 2 cups flour
- ¼ cup brown sugar
- 1 teaspoon pumpkin pie spice
- ½ teaspoon baking soda
- ½ teaspoon salt
- ¼ cup butter
- 1 egg yolk
- ⅓ cup molasses
- ¼ cup milk

Instructions

1 Preheat oven to 400 F.

2 In a large bowl, stir together flour, brown sugar, pumpkin pie spice, baking soda and salt.

3 Using a pastry blender, cut in butter until mixture resembles coarse crumbs.

4 In a small bowl, whisk together egg yolk, molasses and milk. Add to dry ingredients, stirring just until it is combined.

5 Place dough on an ungreased baking sheet and form into a circle; score with a knife to form 8 triangles.

6 Bake for 12 to 15 minutes. Remove from oven and cool on a wire rack for 5 minutes, then cut all the way through to form 8 triangular scones.

Chocolate Chip Pumpkin Bread

All-American • Easy • Family Favorite

Often, fresh fruits have a higher nutrient content than canned, but not when it comes to pumpkin.

PREP *15 minutes*

TOTAL *1 hour 20 minutes; 20 minutes inactive*

YIELD *16 servings*

Ingredients

- 4 eggs
- 2 cups sugar
- 2 cups canned pumpkin
- 1½ cups vegetable oil
- 3 cups all-purpose flour
- 1 teaspoon cinnamon
- 1 teaspoon salt
- 1 teaspoon baking soda
- 1 cup semisweet chocolate chips

Instructions

1 Preheat oven to 350 F. Grease two 8x4-inch loaf pans.

2 In a large bowl, whisk eggs, sugar, pumpkin and oil until blended.

3 Gradually add flour, cinnamon, salt and baking soda and stir just until incorporated. Fold in chocolate chips. Pour into loaf pans.

4 Bake for 60 to 65 minutes or until a toothpick inserted in center comes out clean.

5 Cool on wire rack for 20 minutes.

So Festive for the Holidays!

Orange Cranberry Apple Bread

TIP
Don't skip the orange zest; it adds an irresistible citrus-y aroma.

Orange Cranberry Apple Bread

All-American • Easy • Family Favorite

This quick bread is packed with fruity flavor, perfect for breakfast or a snack.

PREP *20 minutes*

TOTAL *1 hour 15 minutes; 1 hour 10 minutes inactive*

YIELD *16 servings*

Ingredients

2¾ cups all-purpose flour

⅔ cup sugar

⅔ cup brown sugar

1 teaspoon salt

½ teaspoon cinnamon

1 egg

1 cup milk

½ cup orange juice

¼ cup vegetable oil

1 tablespoon grated orange zest

2 cups fresh cranberries

1 Granny Smith apple, peeled, cored and chopped

Instructions

1 Preheat oven to 350 F. Grease two 8x4-inch loaf pans.

2 In a large bowl combine flour, sugars, salt and cinnamon.

3 In another bowl, whisk together egg, milk, orange juice, oil and orange zest.

4 Stir into dry ingredients just until combined.

5 Fold in cranberries and apple.

6 Pour into prepared loaf pans and bake for 50 to 55 minutes or until a toothpick inserted in center comes out clean.

7 Let cool for 10 minutes on wire rack and then remove from pans and place on wire rack to cool for 1 hour before serving.

Morning Glory Muffins

Easy • Healthy

Yes, muffins can be good for you! This one is loaded with carrots, fruit and nuts.

PREP *30 minutes*

TOTAL *53 minutes*

YIELD *16 muffins*

Ingredients

3 large eggs

½ cup packed dark brown sugar

¼ cup honey

⅓ cup canola oil

⅓ cup unsweetened applesauce

⅓ cup unsweetened apple juice

1 teaspoon vanilla extract

2 cups whole-wheat flour

2 teaspoons baking soda

2 teaspoons apple pie spice

½ teaspoon salt

2 cups shredded carrots

1 cup grated apple

½ cup golden raisins

½ cup chopped pecans

Instructions

1 Preheat oven to 425 F. Line 2 muffin pans with a total of 16 paper liners and set aside.

2 In a medium bowl, whisk together eggs, brown sugar, honey, oil, applesauce, apple juice and vanilla.

3 Add flour, baking soda, apple pie spice and salt and stir until incorporated. Fold in carrots, apple, raisins and pecans until just combined.

4 Spoon batter into prepared pan, filling muffin cups to top.

5 Bake for 5 minutes at 425 F, then reduce oven temperature to 350 F. Bake for an additional 18 minutes or until a toothpick inserted in center comes out clean.

6 Allow muffins to cool for 10 minutes in pan, then transfer to a wire rack to cool until ready to eat.

7 Cover leftover muffins and store at room temperature for 2 days or in refrigerator for 1 week.

Breads, Rolls & Biscuits

IS THERE ANYTHING MORE ENTICING THAN A FRESH LOAF OF BREAD OR BATCH OF BISCUITS PULLED PIPING HOT FROM THE OVEN? IF YOU'VE NEVER WORKED WITH YEAST BEFORE, THESE RECIPES MAKE IT FOOLPROOF.

Cinnamon Rolls,
p. 106

TIP
Make this recipe dairy-free by subbing in coconut, rice, potato or soy powdered milk.

Five Grain Bread

Family Favorite • Healthy

Nothing smells better than fresh bread baking in the oven. This recipe is no exception.

PREP *20 minutes*

TOTAL *1 hour 10 minutes; 2 hours inactive*

YIELD *1 (9-inch-long) loaf*

Ingredients

- 3 cups all-purpose flour
- 1 tablespoon vital wheat gluten
- 1 cup five grain blend
- 2 teaspoons salt
- 2 tablespoons sugar
- 2 teaspoons instant yeast
- ⅓ cup dry nonfat milk
- 1¼ cups lukewarm water
- 3 tablespoons vegetable oil

Instructions

1 Grease a 9x5-inch loaf pan.

2 In bowl of an electric mixer fitted with a dough hook, place all ingredients and mix until dough is smooth.

3 Place dough in a greased bowl; cover and let rise 1 hour.

4 Turn dough out onto an oiled surface and shape into a log.

5 Place dough in prepared loaf pan, cover and let rise 1 hour.

6 Toward end of rising time, preheat oven to 350 F.

7 Bake bread for 35 to 40 minutes, or until golden brown.

8 Remove from pan and cool on a wire rack.

Cinnamon Rolls

All-American • Company-Worthy

Make weekend or holiday mornings special with these delicious rolls.

PREP *25 minutes*

TOTAL *45 minutes; 25 minutes inactive*

YIELD *9 rolls*

Rolls

2¾ cups all-purpose flour
  3 tablespoons sugar
  1 teaspoon salt
  1 package instant yeast
  ½ cup water
  ¼ cup milk
  2 tablespoons plus ¼ cup softened butter, divided
  1 egg, beaten
  2 tablespoons cinnamon
  ¼ cup brown sugar

Icing

  1 cup powdered sugar
  1 teaspoon vanilla
  3 tablespoons milk

For the rolls

1 In a large bowl, stir together flour, sugar, salt and yeast. Set aside.

2 In a small microwave-safe bowl, place water, milk and 2 tablespoons butter; microwave for 40 seconds, until butter is melted. Stir to combine.

3 Stir butter mixture into flour mixture. Add egg and knead by hand until dough is no longer sticky.

4 Place dough in a greased bowl and let rest 5 minutes.

5 Roll dough out into a 15x9-inch rectangle. Spread with remaining ¼ cup softened butter. Sprinkle with cinnamon and brown sugar.

6 Roll up dough and slice into 9 rounds.

7 Preheat oven to 200 F. Lightly grease a 9-inch square pan, place rolls in pan and cover with foil.

8 Turn oven off and place rolls in it to rise for 20 minutes.

9 Remove foil, turn oven up to 375 F and bake rolls for 15 to 20 minutes.

For the icing

1 In a small bowl, mix powdered sugar, vanilla and milk.

2 Drizzle over warm rolls.

No-Knead Cranberry Walnut Bread

All-American • Holiday Classic

This yeast bread is airier and less sweet than the traditional quick version.

PREP *30 minutes*

TOTAL *1 hour; 13 hours inactive*

YIELD *8 servings*

Ingredients

3¼ cups all-purpose flour
  1 teaspoon salt
  ½ teaspoon instant yeast
  ¾ cup chopped walnuts
  ¾ cups dried cranberries
  1 tablespoon honey
1½ cups warm water

Instructions

1 In a large bowl, combine first 6 ingredients. Stir in warm water and gently shape into a ball. (The dough will be sticky.)

2 Cover with plastic wrap and leave to rise at room temperature for 12 hours or until doubled in size.

3 Turn dough onto a lightly floured surface and shape into a loaf.

4 Transfer dough onto a baking sheet lined with parchment paper. Cover with plastic wrap and let rest for 30 minutes.

5 Preheat oven to 450 F. Bake for 25 to 30 minutes.

6 Let cool on wire rack for 30 minutes before serving.

Cinnamon Rolls

No-Knead
Cranberry
Walnut Bread

*Goat Cheese
Biscuits*

Goat Cheese Biscuits

Company-Worthy • Easy

These biscuits are delicious on their own, or serve with smoked salmon or ham for a sophisticated starter for a brunch or dinner party.

PREP *15 minutes*

TOTAL *25 minutes*

YIELD *1 dozen*

Ingredients

- 2 cups all-purpose flour
- 1 tablespoon baking powder
- 1 teaspoon salt
- ¼ cup cold butter, cubed
- ¾ cup buttermilk
- 1 (5-ounce) log goat cheese, cubed

Instructions

1 Preheat oven to 475 F. Coat a baking sheet with cooking spray.

2 In large bowl, combine flour, baking powder and salt.

3 Using a pastry blender, cut in butter cubes until pieces are pea-sized.

4 Stir in buttermilk. Fold in goat cheese (it's OK if there are chunks) then knead dough into a ball.

5 Place on a floured surface and flatten to a thickness of ¾ inch.

6 With a round cookie or biscuit cutter, cut into 2-inch circles.

7 Place on prepared baking sheet and bake for 10 to 12 minutes.

Pepper Jack Biscuits

Company-Worthy • Family Favorite

These biscuits are unbelievably easy to make in just 20 minutes. You won't be able to eat just one!

PREP *10 minutes*

TOTAL *20 minutes*

YIELD *10 servings*

Biscuits

- 2 cups all-purpose flour
- 1 tablespoon sugar
- 1 tablespoon baking powder
- 1 teaspoon salt
- ½ teaspoon cayenne pepper
- 1 cup buttermilk
- ½ cup butter, melted
- 1½ cups pepper jack cheese, shredded

Topping

- ¼ cup butter, melted
- 1 tablespoon chopped fresh chives

For the biscuits

1 Preheat oven to 450 F. Line a large baking sheet with parchment paper.

2 In a large bowl, stir together flour, sugar, baking powder, salt and cayenne pepper. Make a well in middle.

3 In another bowl, whisk together buttermilk and butter. Pour into well and slowly incorporate into flour mixture. Fold in cheese.

4 Using a ¼-cup measure, scoop batter evenly onto prepared baking sheet. Bake for 10 to 12 minutes or until golden brown.

For the topping

1 Stir butter and chives together.

2 Brush tops of biscuits with butter mixture and serve immediately.

TIP
You can usually find active dry yeast in the baking aisle of the grocery store.

Cinnamon Raisin Babka

Cinnamon Raisin Babka

Company-Worthy • Family Favorite

This sweet-smelling bread will be your newest obsession.

PREP *50 minutes*

TOTAL *1 hour 45 minutes; 13 hours inactive*

YIELD *8 servings*

Dough

- 1 cup whole milk, warmed
- 2 tablespoons active dry yeast
- 4 cups all-purpose flour
- ¼ cup sugar
- 2 eggs
- ½ cup butter, softened

Filling

- 1 cup brown sugar
- 4 teaspoons cinnamon
- 3 tablespoons all-purpose flour
- ½ cup butter, melted
- 1 cup raisins

Topping

- ¼ cup all-purpose flour
- 1 teaspoon cinnamon
- 2 tablespoons brown sugar
- 2 tablespoons cold butter, cubed
- 1 egg, beaten

For the dough

1 In a small bowl, combine milk and yeast. Let sit for 5 minutes until mixture is bubbly.

2 In bowl of a standing mixer fitted with a dough hook, combine flour, sugar and eggs.

3 Add yeast mixture to dry ingredients and process until combined.

4 Add butter and mix until fully incorporated.

5 Add cold water, one tablespoon at a time, until dough comes together.

6 Cover dough and let rise in refrigerator for 12 hours.

For the filling

Once dough has risen, in a medium bowl, stir together brown sugar, cinnamon, flour and butter.

For the topping

1 In a medium bowl, stir together flour, cinnamon and brown sugar.

2 Add cubed butter and incorporate it into dry ingredients with your fingers.

To assemble

1 Preheat oven to 350 F. Generously coat a 9x5-inch loaf pan with cooking spray.

2 Divide dough into two balls. Roll each ball into a ¼-inch-thick rectangle.

3 Spread cinnamon filling over dough. Sprinkle raisins on top.

4 Roll each rectangle up tightly, starting with shorter side.

5 Cut both dough rolls in half lengthwise, then pinch ends of all four together and braid them. Pinch other ends together.

6 Place braided dough in prepared loaf pan. Brush with egg, then sprinkle with topping.

7 Cover loaf and let rise for 1 hour.

8 Bake for 40 to 50 minutes. Cool on wire rack.

Sour Cream Butter Rolls

Easy • Family Favorite

Curious why there is no salt in this recipe? That's because self-rising flour has salt in it already.

PREP *10 minutes*

TOTAL *25 minutes*

YIELD *3 dozen*

Ingredients

- 2 cups self-rising flour
- 1 cup butter, melted
- 8 ounces sour cream

Instructions

1 Preheat oven to 400 F. Coat 36 cups of 2 mini muffin pans with cooking spray.

2 In a large bowl, combine all ingredients and spoon batter into prepared pans.

3 Bake for 14 to 16 minutes. Serve warm.

Sour Cream Butter Rolls

Garlic Herb Bread

Company-Worthy • Family Favorite

This aromatic variation on a no-knead bread takes some time to make, but it's well worth it!

PREP 30 minutes

TOTAL 1 hour 15 minutes; 10 hours inactive

YIELD 12 servings

Ingredients

- 3 cups all-purpose flour
- 1 teaspoon salt
- ¾ teaspoon active dry yeast
- 1½ cups warm water
- 1 tablespoon minced garlic
- 1 tablespoon fresh thyme leaves
- 2 teaspoons finely chopped fresh parsley
- 2 tablespoons extra-virgin olive oil
- 1 teaspoon coarse kosher salt

Instructions

1 In a large bowl, whisk together flour, salt and yeast. Make a well in middle and add warm water, slowly incorporating it into flour mixture until a dough forms.

2 Cover and let rise in a warm place until doubled in size, 6 to 8 hours.

3 In a small bowl, stir together garlic, thyme and parsley.

4 Dust a piece of parchment paper with flour and place dough on it. Spread garlic-herb mixture over dough. Fold dough in half then press down a bit. Repeat 4 times to incorporate ingredients, then shape into a ball.

5 Cover with a towel and let rise again until nearly doubled in size, 1 to 1½ hours.

6 Preheat oven to 450 F for 30 minutes. Place a large Dutch oven and its lid in oven while oven is heating.

7 Remove Dutch oven from oven. Use parchment paper to lift dough into hot Dutch oven.

8 Drizzle loaf with olive oil and sprinkle with kosher salt.

9 Cover and bake for 30 minutes, then remove lid and bake until bread is browned, about 15 more minutes. Let cool 30 minutes before slicing.

TIP
You can also make a fancier version of these twists with frozen puff pastry dough that's been defrosted.

Pumpkin Pie Twists

Easy • Family Favorite • Holiday Classic

These super simple twists are reminiscent of pumpkin pie.

PREP 10 minutes

TOTAL 25 minutes

YIELD 9 twists

Ingredients

- ½ (15.1-ounce) package refrigerated pie crust
- 1 teaspoon pumpkin pie spice
- 3 tablespoons sugar
- 2 tablespoons melted butter

Instructions

1 Preheat oven to 400 F. Coat a baking sheet with cooking spray.

2 In a small bowl, stir together pumpkin pie spice and sugar.

3 Unroll pie crust on a floured surface. Brush with melted butter. Sprinkle with sugar mixture.

4 Cut into 9 long strips of dough. Twist each and place on baking sheet.

5 Bake for 12 to 15 minutes or until golden brown.

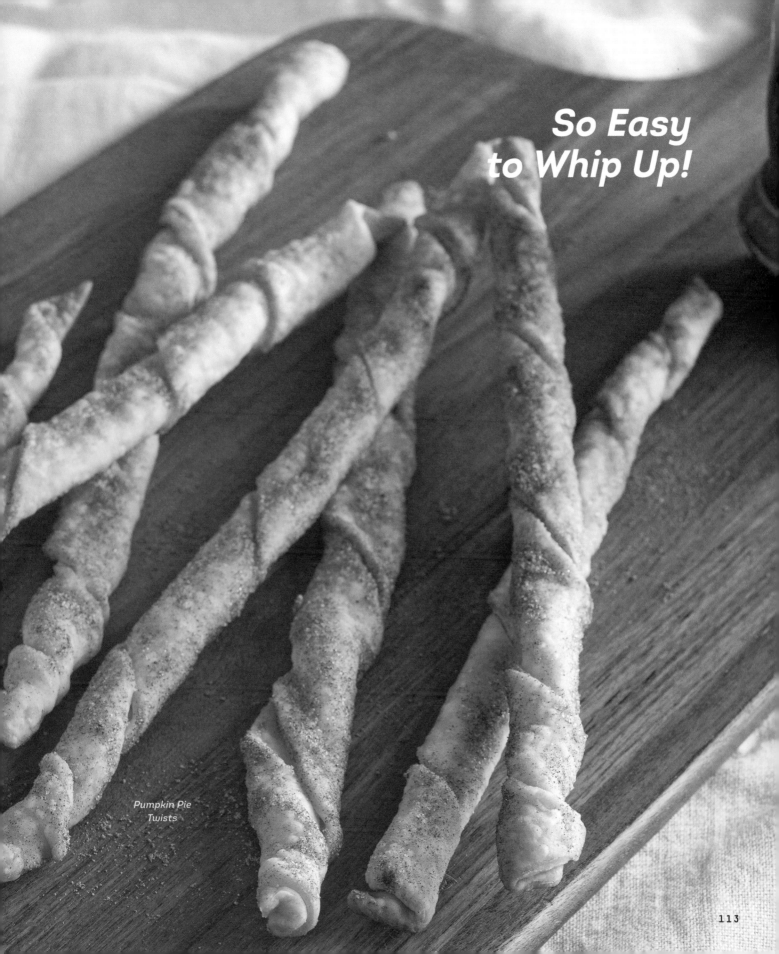

So Easy to Whip Up!

Pumpkin Pie
Twists

TIP
To avoid tough biscuits, mix the dough just until ingredients are combined.

Drop Biscuits

Drop Biscuits

Company-Worthy • Easy • Family Favorite

This recipe is so simple, you can whip these biscuits up while you cook the rest of the meal.

PREP *5 minutes*

TOTAL *15 minutes*

YIELD *18 biscuits*

Ingredients

- 2 cups flour
- 1 tablespoon baking powder
- 1 teaspoon sugar
- ½ teaspoon salt
- ½ cup butter, melted
- ¼ cup water

Instructions

1 Preheat oven to 400 F. Line a large baking sheet with parchment paper.

2 In a large bowl, combine all ingredients.

3 Drop by tablespoonfuls onto prepared baking sheet.

4 Bake for 10 minutes or until golden.

Rosemary Focaccia

Company-Worthy • Easy

Refrigerated pizza dough means this bread is super quick to make. Serve it with some good olive oil for dipping.

PREP *15 minutes*

TOTAL *35 minutes*

YIELD *8 servings*

Ingredients

- 1 pound refrigerated pizza dough
- 2 tablespoons olive oil
- 1 tablespoon rosemary leaves
- ½ teaspoon flaky sea salt

Instructions

1 Preheat oven to 350 F. Lightly grease a sheet pan.

2 Pat dough into rectangle and place on prepared pan.

3 Drizzle with olive oil and sprinkle with rosemary and sea salt.

4 Bake for 20 minutes.

Rosemary
Focaccia

Four-Ingredient
Biscuits

Make Meals Yummy With a Warm Biscuit

TIP
Southern cooks swear by self-rising flour. Make it by adding 1½ teaspoons of baking powder and ¼ teaspoon of salt to 1 cup of all-purpose flour.

Four-Ingredient Biscuits

Easy • Family Favorite

There is no excuse not to have fresh bread on the table with this simple recipe.

PREP *5 minutes*

TOTAL *20 minutes*

YIELD *1 dozen*

Ingredients

- 3 cups self-rising flour
- ¼ cup mayonnaise
- 1 cup whole milk
- 1 teaspoon sugar

Instructions

1 Preheat oven to 400 F. Coat a muffin tin with cooking spray.

2 In a medium bowl, mix all ingredients.

3 Fill muffin cups ⅔ of the way full.

4 Bake for 10 to 12 minutes or until golden brown.

Easy Yeast Rolls

Company-Worthy • Family Favorite

If you've never worked with yeast before, this is a good recipe to start with.

PREP *25 minutes*

TOTAL *35 minutes; 1 hour inactive*

YIELD *8 servings*

Ingredients

- 2 tablespoons butter, melted
- ¼ cup sugar
- 1 cup hot water
- 1 (¼-ounce) package active dry yeast
- 1 egg, beaten
- 1 teaspoon salt
- 2¼ cups all-purpose flour

Instructions

1 Grease 8 cups of a regular muffin tin.

2 In a large bowl, stir together butter, sugar and hot water. Allow to cool to lukewarm, then whisk in yeast until dissolved. Let sit for 5 minutes until bubbly.

3 Stir in egg, salt and flour. Cover and leave dough to rise until it doubles in size about 30 minutes.

4 Divide dough into 8 pieces and place in prepared muffin cups and allow to rise again until doubled in size, 30 minutes.

5 While dough is rising, preheat oven to 425 F. Bake for 10 minutes, or until golden brown on top.

Cobblers, Crisps & Crumbles

THESE RUSTIC, UNPRETENTIOUS DESSERTS ARE SOME OF OUR FAVORITE WAYS TO ENJOY THE SEASON'S BOUNTY. ADD A SCOOP OF VANILLA ICE CREAM AND YOU'LL WANT FALL TO LAST FOREVER.

Pear Cobbler,
p. 127

Your New Fall Classic Is Here

Sweet Potato, Pear and Fig Crumble

Company-Worthy • Easy

This dessert showcases the best flavors of fall.

PREP *20 minutes*

TOTAL *1 hour*

YIELD *8 servings*

Ingredients

- 2 (15.75-ounce) cans sweet potatoes in syrup, undrained
- 2 pears, peeled, cored and chopped
- 1 (8-ounce) container dried figs, quartered
- ¼ cup plus 1 tablespoon maple syrup, divided
- 1 teaspoon lemon juice
- ½ teaspoon cinnamon
- 1 cup old-fashioned oats
- 1 cup chopped pecans
- ⅓ cup flour
- ⅓ cup brown sugar
- ¼ teaspoon nutmeg
- ⅓ cup butter, melted
- Garnish: vanilla ice cream

Instructions

1 Preheat oven to 350 F. Lightly coat an 8-inch baking dish with cooking spray.

2 Drain sweet potatoes, reserving ¼ cup syrup.

3 In a large bowl, stir together sweet potatoes, reserved syrup, pears, figs, ¼ cup maple syrup, lemon juice and cinnamon. Pour mixture into prepared dish.

4 In a separate bowl, combine oats, pecans, flour, brown sugar, nutmeg, butter and remaining maple syrup. Sprinkle over sweet potato mixture.

5 Bake 35 to 40 minutes. Serve with vanilla ice cream, if desired.

TIP
For a less-expensive alternative to Honeycrisp, try Jazz, Pink Lady or Ambrosia varieties.

Apple Crumble

All-American • Easy • Family Favorite

Honeycrisp apples remain firm (and delicious!) even when baked.

PREP *15 minutes*

TOTAL *1 hour*

YIELD *8 servings*

Ingredients

- 7 Honeycrisp apples, peeled cored and cubed
- 1 tablespoon lemon zest
- 2 tablespoons lemon juice
- 3 tablespoons light brown sugar, divided
- 1 teaspoon cinnamon, divided
- ¼ teaspoon salt
- ½ cup old-fashioned oats
- ½ cup chopped pecans
- 2 tablespoons flour
- ¼ cup cold butter, cut into ¼-inch pieces

Instructions

1 Preheat oven to 350 F. Lightly coat a 9-inch baking dish with cooking spray.

2 In a large bowl, toss together apples, lemon zest and juice, 2 tablespoons brown sugar, ½ teaspoon cinnamon and salt. Let stand 10 minutes. Place apple mixture into prepared baking dish.

3 Meanwhile, in a medium bowl, stir together oats, pecans, flour, remaining 1 tablespoon brown sugar and remaining ½ teaspoon cinnamon. Add butter, and using your hands, rub it into flour mixture until it comes together into large clumps.

4 Top apples with oat mixture.

5 Bake for 45 minutes or until bubbly and browned.

Best Served Warm!

TIP
You can also bake this in a cast-iron skillet for a rustic-looking dessert.

Sweet Potato Cobbler

Easy • Family Favorite • Holiday Classic

This tastes like Thanksgiving in every bite, but it's so good you will want to make it all year long.

PREP *20 minutes*

TOTAL *45 minutes*

YIELD *8 servings*

Ingredients

- 1 (15-ounce) can sweet potatoes in syrup, undrained
- 2 cups plus 1 tablespoon sugar, divided
- ¼ cup flour
- 1 tablespoon pumpkin pie spice
- ½ cup butter
- ¼ cup chopped pecans
- ½ (14.1-ounce) package refrigerated pie crust
- 2 tablespoons heavy cream

Instructions

1 Preheat oven to 400 F. Lightly coat a 9-inch baking dish with cooking spray. Drain sweet potatoes, reserving syrup.

2 In a medium saucepan over medium heat, stir together reserved syrup, 2 cups sugar, flour and pumpkin pie spice. Whisk sugar until dissolved. Add butter and stir until melted.

3 Slice sweet potatoes and arrange them and chopped pecans in prepared baking dish. Pour syrup mixture over them.

4 Place pie crust over sweet potatoes. Crimp and fold edges to cover sweet potatoes. Brush with cream and sprinkle with remaining 1 tablespoon sugar.

5 Bake for 20 to 25 minutes or until crust is browned.

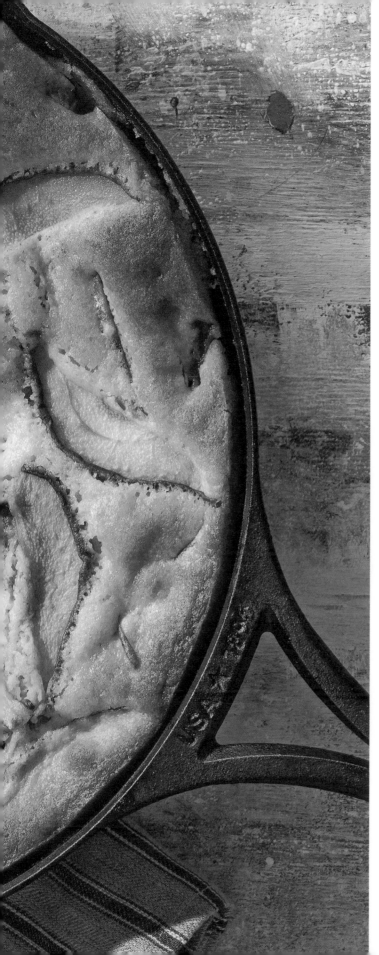

TIP
Cobblers can be made with almost any fruit—try apples, peaches, plums or berries.

Pear Cobbler

All-American • Easy •Family Favorite

Don't refrigerate your red Anjou pears! They taste best when allowed to ripen at room temperature.

PREP *20 minutes*

TOTAL *1 hour 30 minutes*

YIELD *12 servings*

Ingredients

- 6 large red Anjou pears, peeled, cored and cut into ¼-inch slices
- ⅓ cup light brown sugar
- 1 teaspoon grated ginger
- 1 teaspoon cornstarch
- 1 teaspoon cinnamon
- 1 cup sugar
- ⅓ cup canola oil
- 2 teaspoons vanilla extract
- 2 eggs
- ½ cup milk
- 1⅓ cups flour
- 1 tablespoon baking powder
- ½ teaspoon salt

Instructions

1 Preheat oven to 350 F. Lightly coat a 12-inch cast-iron skillet with cooking spray.

2 In a large bowl, toss together pears, brown sugar, ginger, cornstarch and cinnamon. Spread evenly in bottom of a prepared skillet.

3 In bowl of a standing mixer set on high speed, beat sugar, oil, vanilla and eggs until fluffy.

4 Add milk, then gradually add flour, baking powder and salt until just incorporated. Pour batter evenly over pears.

5 Bake 50 minutes to 1 hour or until toothpick inserted in center of cake comes out clean.

6 Cool 10 minutes before serving.

TIP
No cookies on hand? Try using other toppings like granola, chopped pecans or chopped walnuts.

Apple Crisp With Oatmeal Cookie Crust

All-American • Easy • Family Favorite

This dessert is topped with crumbled oatmeal cookies, so it's super quick to throw together.

PREP *10 minutes*

TOTAL *1 hour*

YIELD *8 servings*

Ingredients

- 4 Granny Smith apples, peeled, cored and sliced
- 1 tablespoon lemon juice
- ⅓ cup sugar
- ½ cup light brown sugar
- 1 teaspoon apple pie spice
- ¼ cup flour
- 8 oatmeal cookies, crumbled
- ¼ cup butter, cubed
   Garnish: whipped cream, dusting of cinnamon

Instructions

1 Preheat oven to 375 F. Lightly coat a 2-quart baking dish with cooking spray.

2 In a large bowl, combine apples, lemon juice, sugars, apple pie spice and flour. Place apple mixture in prepared baking dish.

3 Top with crumbled oatmeal cookies and dot with butter.

4 Bake for 45 to 50 minutes, or until bubbly and browned.

5 Let cool and top with whipped cream and cinnamon, if desired.

So Yummy on a Cool Fall Night!

TIP Place pears in a brown bag to speed ripening.

Pear Brown Sugar Crumble

Easy • Family Favorite

Pears make a nice change from apples in this dessert; brown sugar adds a luscious caramel-esque flavor.

PREP *15 minutes*

TOTAL *55 minutes*

YIELD *6 servings*

Ingredients

- 1 cup flour
- ½ cup light brown sugar
- ½ teaspoon cinnamon
- ¼ teaspoon nutmeg
- 6 tablespoons butter, softened
- 4 pears, peeled and sliced
  Garnish: whipped cream

Instructions

1 Preheat oven to 375 F. Lightly coat an 8-inch square baking pan with cooking spray.

2 In a medium bowl, stir together flour, brown sugar, cinnamon and nutmeg. With a pastry blender, cut in butter until mixture resembles coarse crumbs.

3 Arrange pear slices in bottom of prepared baking pan. Sprinkle crumb mixture over pears.

4 Bake 35 to 40 minutes or until browned. Let cool and top with whipped cream, if desired.

TIP
Cranberries are a rich source of vitamin C and have 4.6 grams of fiber per cup.

Cranberry Apple Crisp

All-American • Easy • Holiday Classic

Two fall staples—apples and cranberries—double the impact of this sweet-and-tart crisp.

PREP *15 minutes*

TOTAL *1 hour 10 minutes*

YIELD *8 servings*

Ingredients

- 2 cups cranberries
- 3 cups peeled, chopped apples
- 1 cup sugar
- ¾ cup flour, divided
- 2 cups old-fashioned oats
- ½ cup brown sugar
- ½ cup butter, melted
- ⅓ cup chopped pecans
- Garnish: vanilla ice cream

Instructions

1 Preheat oven to 350 F. Coat an 11x7-inch baking dish with cooking spray.

2 In a large bowl, combine cranberries, apples, sugar and ¼ cup flour. Pour mixture into prepared baking dish.

3 In the same bowl, combine oats, remaining ½ cup flour, brown sugar, butter and pecans. Sprinkle over apple mixture.

4 Bake for 50 to 55 minutes or until browned and bubbly.

5 Let cool and top with vanilla ice cream, if desired.

Top With
Vanilla
Ice Cream

A Quickie Sub for Pumpkin Pie

Pumpkin Crumble

All-American • Company-Worthy • Holiday Classic

The luscious taste of pumpkin pie without having to make
a crust? Sign us up!

PREP *15 minutes*

TOTAL *1 hour 5 minutes*

YIELD *12 servings*

Ingredients

  2 (15-ounce) cans pumpkin puree
  1 cup heavy cream
  1 cup half-and-half
1½ cups sugar
  3 eggs
  2 teaspoons pumpkin pie spice
  ½ teaspoon salt
  1 cup old-fashioned oats
  1 cup light brown sugar
  ¾ cup flour
  1 stick butter, melted
     Garnish: whipped cream

Instructions

1 Preheat oven to 350 F. Lightly coat a 13x9-baking dish
with cooking spray.

2 In a large bowl, whisk together pumpkin puree, heavy
cream, half-and-half, sugar, eggs, pumpkin pie spice and salt
until well combined. Spoon into baking dish.

3 In a medium bowl, combine oats, brown sugar,
flour and butter until crumbly. Sprinkle on top of
pumpkin mixture.

4 Bake about 50 minutes or until browned. Let cool and
serve with whipped cream, if desired.

Desserts

THESE INVENTIVE RECIPES WILL MAKE FOR A
SPECTACULAR CONCLUSION TO A DINNER PARTY, POTLUCK,
FAMILY GET-TOGETHER OR ANY SPECIAL OCCASION.

Cinnamon
Swirl Dessert
Coffee Cake,
p. 148

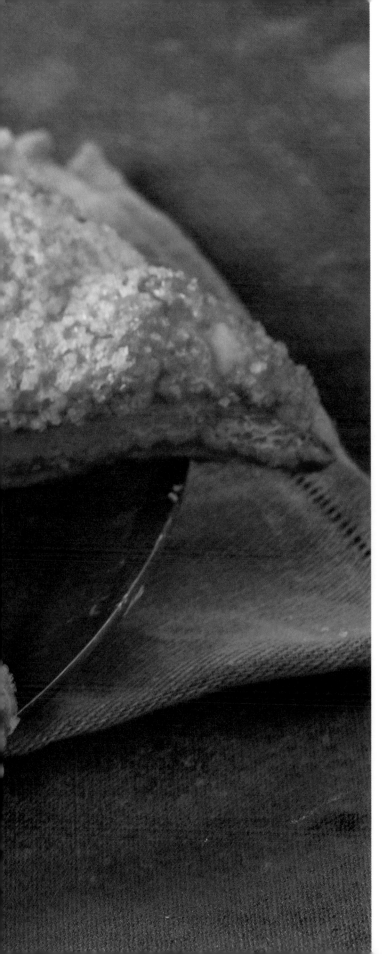

TIP
Sanding sugar has larger crystals than granulated, but you can also sub in regular sugar.

Pear Turnovers

All-American • Company-Worthy • Easy

Frozen puff pastry make these turnovers a cinch to whip up.

PREP *15 minutes*

TOTAL *45 minutes*

YIELD *4 servings*

Ingredients

- 1   firm pear, peeled, cored and chopped
- 1   tablespoon honey
- ½   teaspoon all-purpose flour
- 1   frozen puff pastry sheet, thawed
- 1   egg white, beaten
- 2   teaspoons sanding sugar

Instructions

1 Preheat oven to 350 F. Line a baking sheet with parchment paper.

2 In a small bowl, toss pear, honey and flour until well combined.

3 Unroll puff pastry and cut it into four squares. Place an equal amount of pear mixture in middle of each square.

4 Dip fingers in water; moisten edges of pastry squares. Fold pastry over pears to form a triangle. Press edges together, then use a fork to press gently along edges to seal.

5 Brush turnovers with egg white and sprinkle with sugar.

6 Bake for 25 to 30 minutes, until golden brown.

Gingerbread Doughnuts

All-American • Family Favorite • Holiday Classic

It's not just for cookies and cakes! Give doughnuts a seasonal flair with a bit of gingerbread spice.

PREP *15 minutes*

TOTAL *30 minutes*

YIELD *1 dozen*

Doughnuts

- 2 tablespoons butter, melted
- ¼ cup brown sugar
- ¼ cup molasses
- 1 egg
- ½ cup milk
- 3 tablespoons sour cream
- 1¼ cups flour
- 1 teaspoon cinnamon
- ¾ teaspoon ground ginger
- ⅛ teaspoon ground cloves
- ½ teaspoon baking powder
- ¼ teaspoon baking soda
- ¼ teaspoon salt

Coating

- ¼ cup butter
- ⅓ cup powdered sugar
- ½ teaspoon cinnamon
- ½ teaspoon ground ginger

For the doughnuts

1 Preheat oven to 350 F. Grease two, 6-count doughnut pans and set aside.

2 In bowl of an electric mixer on medium speed, cream butter and brown sugar until combined. Beat in molasses and egg, then add milk and sour cream.

3 On low speed, gradually add flour, cinnamon, ginger, cloves, baking powder, baking soda and salt and mix until just incorporated. Avoid overmixing.

4 Spoon batter into doughnut pans.

5 Bake for 13 to 15 minutes, or until doughnuts spring back when lightly touched.

For the coating

1 In a microwave-safe bowl, microwave butter until melted.

2 In a separate shallow bowl, whisk together powdered sugar, cinnamon and ginger.

3 While doughnuts are still warm, dip into butter, then roll in sugar mixture. Serve immediately.

Caramel Custard

Company-Worthy • Easy

This simple yet elegant dessert can be made any night.

PREP *15 minutes*

TOTAL *1 hour*

YIELD *8 servings*

Ingredients

- 1½ cups sugar, divided
- 6 eggs
- 3 cups milk
- 2 teaspoons vanilla extract

Instructions

1 Preheat oven to 350 F.

2 In a heavy skillet over medium heat, cook ¾ cup sugar, stirring frequently, until sugar turns golden.

3 Pour into bottoms of eight, 6-ounce ramekins, tilting to coat bottoms; let stand for 10 minutes.

4 In a large bowl, beat remaining ¾ cup sugar, eggs, milk and vanilla until blended. Divide between ramekins.

5 Place ramekins in a large roasting pan. Pour boiling water into pan so it comes halfway up sides of ramekins.

6 Bake for 40 to 45 minutes, or until a knife inserted in center of custard comes out clean.

7 Remove ramekins from roasting pan; let cool on wire rack.

8 Unmold by running a knife around rim of ramekin and invert onto dessert place. Serve warm or chilled.

Gingerbread Doughnuts

So Much Yummier Than Store-Bought!

Caramel Custard

TIP
No ramekins on hand? Heat-resistant tea cups work just as well!

Apple Cider Fritters

Apple Cider Fritters

All-American • Family Favorite

These are so delicious, you might not even realize they're baked, not fried!

PREP *15 minutes*

TOTAL *45 minutes*

YIELD *10 servings*

Fritters

- 2 tablespoons butter
- 1½ cups diced Granny Smith apples
- 3 tablespoons brown sugar
- 2 cups all-purpose flour
- 1 tablespoon baking powder
- 1 teaspoon salt
- ½ teaspoon ground cinnamon
- ¼ teaspoon ground nutmeg
- 1 large egg
- ¼ cup sugar
- 1 tablespoon butter, melted
- ½ cup apple cider

Glaze

- ½ cup powdered sugar
- 2 tablespoons apple cider

For the fritters

1 In a large skillet over medium-high heat, melt butter and cook until it turns golden brown, 2 to 3 minutes.

2 Add apples and cook just until they begin to soften, 3 to 4 minutes. Add brown sugar and continue cooking another 2 minutes.

3 Remove from heat. Drain in a strainer and let cool for 10 minutes.

4 Preheat oven to 350 F. Line 2 baking sheets with parchment paper.

5 In a large mixing bowl, combine flour, baking powder, salt, cinnamon and nutmeg.

6 In another bowl, whisk egg, sugar and melted butter together.

7 Add cooled apples and apple cider, then stir in flour mixture just until incorporated.

8 Drop ¼-cup scoops of batter onto prepared baking sheets.

9 Bake for 12 to 15 minutes or until puffed and golden.

For the glaze

1 In a small bowl, whisk powdered sugar and apple cider together.

2 Drizzle over hot fritters and serve immediately.

Millionaire's Shortbread

Company-Worthy • Easy

This version of these rich bars features salted caramel in between layers of chocolate and shortbread.

PREP *20 minutes*

TOTAL *80 to 110 minutes*

YIELD *16 bars*

Crust

- 1½ cups all-purpose flour
- 1 teaspoon kosher salt
- 1 cup (2 sticks) unsalted butter, at room temperature
- ⅓ cup firmly packed light brown sugar
- ⅓ cup granulated sugar
- 1 large egg yolk
- 1 teaspoon vanilla extract

Salted caramel filling

- ¾ cup (1½ sticks) unsalted butter, at room temperature
- ¾ cup firmly packed light brown sugar
- 1 (14-ounce) can sweetened condensed milk
- 1 teaspoon kosher salt
- 8 ounces semisweet chocolate, melted
  Flaky sea salt, for sprinkling

For the crust

1 Preheat oven to 300 F. Coat a 9-inch square baking pan with nonstick cooking spray or butter and line with parchment paper, letting the paper hang slightly over two sides. Spray or butter the parchment.

2 In a small bowl, whisk together flour and salt.

3 In a large bowl, using an electric mixer, beat butter and both sugars together on medium-high speed until light and fluffy, about 3 minutes. Add egg yolk and vanilla and beat until combined. Scrape down the sides of the bowl with a rubber spatula. Add flour mixture and beat on low speed just until combined. Press dough into bottom of prepared pan.

4 Bake until edges are light golden brown, 35 to 45 minutes. Cool completely on wire rack.

For the filling

1 In a medium saucepan set on the stovetop over medium-low heat, combine butter and sugar. Cook, stirring occasionally, until melted. Add condensed milk and salt and bring to a boil, stirring constantly (be careful to avoid caramel splattering), then boil for 1 minute longer without stirring. Remove pan from heat; carefully pour filling over shortbread. Let cool at room temperature for 10 minutes, then refrigerate until set, 30 to 45 minutes.

2 Pour melted chocolate over caramel and sprinkle with sea salt. Refrigerate until set, 15 to 20 minutes. Using parchment paper as handles, remove from pan and cut into bars.

A Treat for Pumpkin Spice Fans!

Baked Pumpkin Pudding

DIY Pumpkin Puree

Baked Pumpkin Pudding

All-American • Easy • Healthy • Holiday Classic

These delectable pumpkin-spiced puddings can be served warm, at room temperature or chilled.

PREP *10 minutes*

TOTAL *55 minutes*

YIELD *8 servings*

Ingredients

- 2 eggs
- 1 (15-ounce) can pumpkin puree
- ¾ cup sugar
- 1 tablespoon honey
- 2 teaspoons pumpkin pie spice
- 1½ cups evaporated milk

Instructions

1 Preheat oven to 425 F. Coat eight (6-ounce) ramekins with cooking spray.

2 In a large bowl, beat eggs, pumpkin puree, sugar, honey and pumpkin pie spice until combined.

3 Whisk in evaporated milk.

4 Pour into prepared ramekins.

5 Place ramekins in a 13x9-inch baking dish. Pour boiling water into pan so it comes halfway up sides of ramekins.

6 Bake, uncovered, for 10 minutes. Reduce heat to 350 F. Bake 25 to 30 minutes longer or until a toothpick inserted in center of one pudding comes out clean.

DIY Pumpkin Puree

All-American • Easy • Holiday Classic

Use fresh puree in place of the canned version for recipes throughout this book.

PREP *10 minutes*

TOTAL *1 hour 10 minutes*

YIELD *8 servings*

Ingredients

- 1 (3-pound) fresh pumpkin, washed

Instructions

1 Preheat oven to 350 F.

2 Cut top off pumpkin and scrape out membranes and seeds. Cut pumpkin into large pieces (leave skin on).

3 Place pumpkin pieces in a roasting pan and pour ½ cup water into bottom of pan.

4 Cover with foil and bake 55 to 60 minutes, or until pumpkin is very soft when pierced with tip of a knife.

5 Let cool, then scrape pulp off skin. Working in batches, place in food processor and pulse until pureed.

6 Refrigerate if using within 3 days. It can also be frozen for up to 12 months.

A New Life for Day-Old Bread

TIP
If you have the time, let the mixture sit in the refrigerator for at least 2 hours to allow the bread to absorb the liquid.

Toffee Pear Bread Pudding

Company-Worthy • Holiday Classic

This stellar dessert is so rich, just a small portion will satisfy your sweet tooth.

PREP *20 minutes*

TOTAL *1 hour; 40 minutes inactive*

YIELD *12 servings*

Pudding

1¾	cups milk
1	cup caramel ice cream topping
¼	cup butter
1	teaspoon cinnamon
½	teaspoon ground ginger
2	eggs
4	cups cubed day-old crusty bread
2	pears, cored and sliced

Topping

½	cup all-purpose flour
½	cup brown sugar
⅓	cup cold butter
⅓	cup toffee bits

For the pudding

1 Preheat oven to 350 F. Grease a 2-quart round casserole dish.

2 In a medium saucepan over low heat, add milk, caramel topping, butter, cinnamon and ginger. Cook, stirring, until butter is melted. Remove from heat; set aside.

3 In a large bowl, whisk eggs; gradually stir in a quarter of milk mixture, then slowly add remaining milk mixture. Fold in bread. Let stand 30 minutes.

4 Gently fold pears into bread-milk mixture. Pour into prepared baking dish and bake for 20 minutes.

For the topping

1 In a small bowl, stir together flour and brown sugar; using a pastry blender or your fingers, cut in butter until crumbly. Stir in toffee bits.

2 Remove bread pudding from oven and sprinkle on topping.

3 Return to oven and bake 20 to 25 minutes more, or until puffed and a knife inserted in center comes out clean.

4 Let stand 10 minutes before serving. Serve warm.

TIP
To prevent coffee cake from drying out, wrap tightly in plastic wrap, then place in a zip-close bag before refrigerating.

Cinnamon Swirl Dessert Coffee Cake

Easy • Family Favorite

This delicious cake isn't just for dessert—try toasting a slice for breakfast or with a coffee.

PREP *20 minutes*

TOTAL *1 hour 20 minutes*

YIELD *10 servings*

Swirl

- ⅓ cup light brown sugar
- ½ cup finely chopped pecans, toasted
- 2 teaspoons ground cinnamon

Cake

- 1 cup sugar
- 2 cups all-purpose flour
- 1 teaspoon baking powder
- ½ teaspoon salt
- 1 large egg
- 1 cup milk
- ⅓ cup butter, melted
- ½ teaspoon vanilla extract

For the swirl

In a small bowl, combine brown sugar, pecans and cinnamon. Set aside.

For the cake

1 Preheat oven to 350 F. Grease a standard loaf pan.

2 Whisk together sugar, flour, baking powder and salt. Make a well in middle of flour mixture.

3 In a separate bowl, beat egg. Stir in milk, butter and vanilla. Pour egg mixture into well in dry ingredients. Stir just until mixed.

4 Pour half of the batter into prepared pan. Sprinkle with half of cinnamon mixture. Repeat with remaining batter and cinnamon mixture. With a wide spatula or knife, swirl mixtures together with an up-and-down circular motion.

5 Bake for 55 to 60 minutes, or until coffee cake is browned and a toothpick inserted in center comes out clean. Cool in pan for about 10 minutes. Remove from pan.

6 Cool completely on a wire rack.

Plum Pudding

Company-Worthy • Holiday Classic

In *A Christmas Carol*, plum pudding was the highlight of the Cratchits' Christmas dinner, as it will be for your family.

PREP *15 minutes*

TOTAL *1 hour; 30 minutes inactive*

YIELD *10 servings*

Ingredients

- 1 cup raisins
- 1 cup dried apricots, chopped
- ½ cup chopped pecans
- 1 tablespoon all-purpose flour
- ½ cup butter, softened
- ¾ cup sugar
- 5 eggs
- 2 teaspoons pumpkin pie spice
- 3 cups bread cubes
  Garnish: whipped cream

Instructions

1 Grease an 8-inch square baking dish.

2 In a medium bowl, mix raisins, apricots and pecans; sprinkle with flour and toss.

3 In a large bowl, using a hand mixer on medium speed, cream together butter and sugar. Beat in eggs, one at a time, until incorporated. Stir in pumpkin pie spice.

4 Fold in raisin mixture, then add bread. Pour into prepared baking dish. Let sit for 30 minutes.

5 Preheat oven to 350 F. Bake for 40 to 45 minutes, or until set. Serve with whipped cream, if desired.

Cinnamon Swirl Dessert Coffee Cake

Apple Walnut Strudel

Easy • Family Favorite

This recipe looks impressive but it's not nearly as complicated to make as it seems.

PREP *25 minutes*

TOTAL *45 minutes*

YIELD *8 servings*

Ingredients

- 1 cup chopped walnuts
- 1 cup canned apple pie filling
- ⅓ cup brown sugar
- 1 teaspoon all-purpose flour
- 1 teaspoon apple pie spice
- 1 sheet puff pastry, thawed
- 1 egg, beaten
- 1 tablespoon coarse sugar

Instructions

1 Preheat oven to 400 F. Line a large baking sheet with parchment paper.

2 In a medium bowl, stir together walnuts, apple pie filling, brown sugar, flour and apple pie spice.

3 Dust a wooden board with flour. Unfold puff pastry. With a lightly floured rolling pin, roll out pastry into a 12-inch by 9-inch rectangle. On each long side, make a series of cuts, 3 inches deep and 1 inch apart (middle 3-inch-wide strip of pastry remains uncut). Transfer to prepared baking sheet.

4 Spread apple mixture over middle third of pastry, leaving about ½ inch uncovered on either end.

5 Beginning at one short end, create braid. Fold first cut strip of dough from left side over filling. Then fold first cut strip on right over it at a slight angle.

6 Continue folding strips of dough over filling, alternating sides, to form a braided pattern.

7 When you get to end, tuck end of dough under braided strips. Repeat on other end.

8 Brush egg mixture on braid. Sprinkle with sugar.

9 Bake about 15 to 20 minutes, or until pastry is golden brown.

10 Let cool for 20 minutes; serve warm or at room temperature.

TIP
If you cook the pears ahead of time, warm them up before serving.

Oven Poached Vanilla Bean Pears

Easy • Healthy

When you don't want something heavy after a large meal, these not-too-sweet pears are perfect.

PREP *10 minutes*

TOTAL *50 minutes*

YIELD *4 servings*

Ingredients

- 4 pears
- 1 tablespoon lemon juice
- ½ cup sugar
- 3 cups water
- 3 cups apple or pear juice
- 1 vanilla bean, split and seeded

Instructions

1 Peel each pear, leaving stem intact.

2 Sprinkle each with lemon juice to avoid browning.

3 Place sugar, water and juice in a Dutch oven over medium heat and stir until sugar has dissolved. Increase heat and simmer for 5 minutes.

4 Add pears to Dutch oven. Split vanilla bean; add pod and seeds. Simmer pears, covered, in liquid for 10 minutes.

5 Meanwhile, preheat oven to 350 F. Place in oven and roast for 20 minutes.

6 Serve pears warm or cooled with a little poaching liquid.

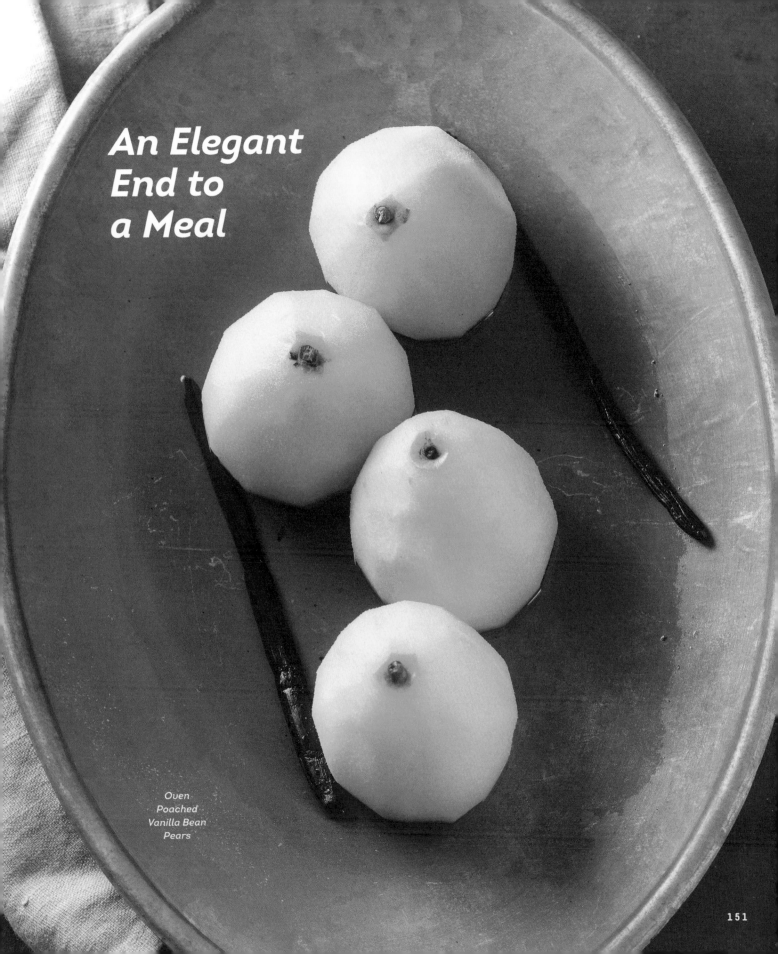

An Elegant End to a Meal

Oven
Poached
Vanilla Bean
Pears

Flavorful, Bite-Size Nuggets

Pumpkin Doughnut Holes

All-American • Easy • Family Favorite

These awesome baked doughnut holes are a fantastic fall treat.

PREP *20 minutes*

TOTAL *30 minutes*

YIELD *2 dozen*

Ingredients

- ⅓ cup vegetable oil
- ½ cup brown sugar
- 1 egg
- 1 teaspoon vanilla extract
- ¾ cup pumpkin puree
- ½ cup milk
- 1¾ cups all-purpose flour
- 2 teaspoons baking powder
- ½ teaspoon salt
- ½ teaspoon plus 2 tablespoons cinnamon, divided
- ½ teaspoon nutmeg
- ½ teaspoon allspice
- ⅔ cup sugar
- ¼ cup butter, melted

Instructions

1 Preheat oven 350 F. Coat a 24-cup mini muffin tin with cooking spray.

2 In a large bowl, whisk together oil, brown sugar, egg, vanilla, pumpkin puree and milk until smooth. Gradually stir in flour, baking powder, salt, ½ teaspoon cinnamon, nutmeg and allspice until just incorporated.

3 Divide batter evenly among muffin cups. Bake for 10 to 12 minutes, or until a toothpick comes out clean.

4 Meanwhile, in a small bowl, combine sugar and remaining 2 tablespoons cinnamon.

5 Remove doughnut holes from oven and cool for 2 minutes.

6 Dip each doughnut hole in melted butter, then roll in cinnamon-sugar mixture. (Mixture will be absorbed as long as doughnuts are still warm.)

TIP
You can also make this in six individual ramekins; bake covered with foil for 20 minutes, then uncover and bake 20 more minutes.

Croissant Bread Pudding With Cranberries and Walnuts

Company-Worthy • Easy • Family Favorite

Day-old croissants will soak up the egg mixture even more than bread for a creamier texture.

PREP *15 minutes*

TOTAL *1 hour 35 minutes; 10 minutes inactive*

YIELD *6 servings*

Ingredients

- 2 large eggs
- 4 large egg yolks
- 1¼ cups half-and-half
- 1¼ cups eggnog
- 1 cup sugar
- 2 teaspoons vanilla extract
- 4 croissants, torn
- ½ cup dried cranberries
- ½ cup chopped walnuts

Instructions

1 Preheat oven to 350 F. Grease a 2-quart baking dish.

2 In a medium bowl, whisk together eggs, egg yolks, half-and-half, eggnog, sugar and vanilla. Set aside.

3 Place croissant pieces in baking dish. Sprinkle dried cranberries and walnuts over top.

4 Pour egg mixture over croissants, pressing down gently; allow to soak for 10 minutes.

5 Place baking dish in a larger pan filled with 1 inch of hot water. Cover both with aluminum foil, tenting foil so it doesn't touch pudding. Cut a few holes in foil to allow steam to escape.

6 Bake for 40 minutes. Uncover and bake for 40 minutes more, or until pudding puffs up and pudding is set.

7 Remove from oven and cool slightly. Serve warm or at room temperature.

A Buttery Delight

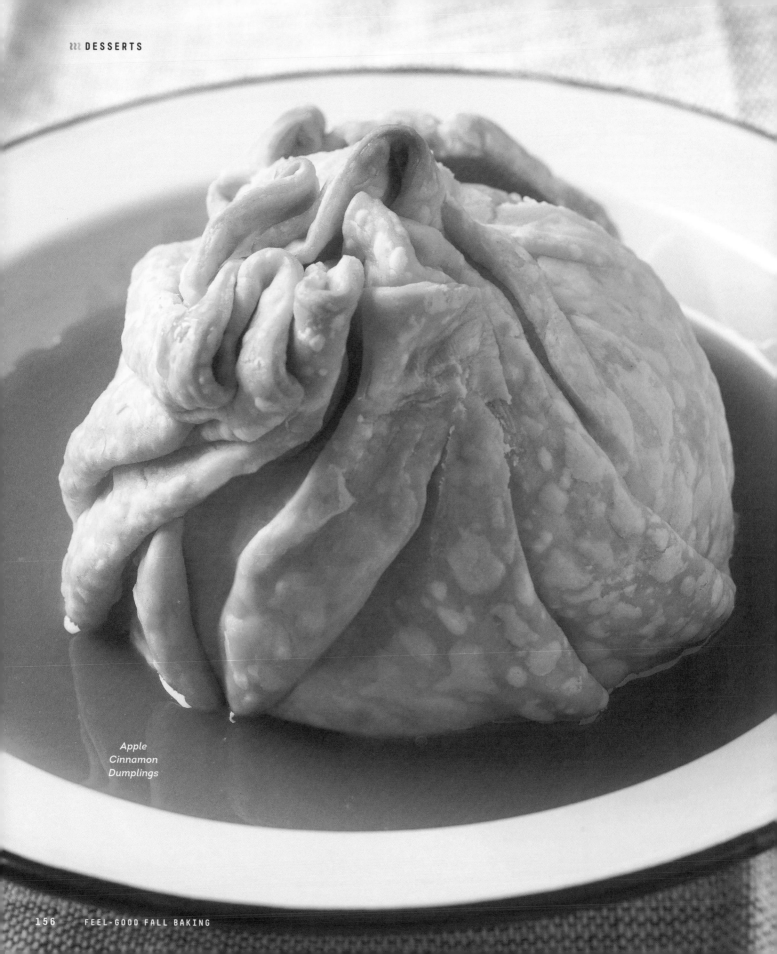

*Apple
Cinnamon
Dumplings*

Apple Cinnamon Dumplings

All-American • Easy • Family Favorite

The aroma of these dumplings while they're baking is irresistible.

PREP *30 minutes*

TOTAL *1 hour 15 minutes*

YIELD *6 servings*

Ingredients

- 1 (14.1-ounce) box refrigerated pie crust
- 6 small apples, peeled and cored
- 1½ cups sugar, divided
- ½ teaspoon ground cinnamon, divided
- 4 tablespoons butter, divided
- 1 cup water

Instructions

1 Preheat oven to 375 F.

2 On a lightly floured surface, roll out pie crusts to form 1 large rectangle. Cut into 6 squares and place an apple in center of each square.

3 In a small bowl, stir together ½ cup sugar and ¼ teaspoon cinnamon.

4 Place 4 teaspoons sugar mixture and ½ teaspoon butter in center of each apple. Moisten edges of pie crust with water; bring four corners together over apples and pinch edges together to seal. Place dumplings in an ungreased 13x9-inch baking dish.

5 In a saucepan over medium-high heat, combine remaining 1 cup sugar, water, remaining 3 tablespoons butter and remaining ¼ teaspoon cinnamon; bring to a boil. Boil 3 minutes; remove from heat and pour over dumplings.

6 Bake until golden brown and apples are tender, about 45 minutes.

Pumpkin Dessert With Vanilla Ice Cream

All-American • Easy • Holiday Classic

Instead of your favorite pumpkin pie, try this new dessert made with a cake mix.

PREP *10 minutes*

TOTAL *1 hour*

YIELD *16 servings*

Ingredients

- 1 (15.25-ounce) package yellow cake mix, divided
- ⅓ cup butter, melted
- 4 eggs, divided
- 1 (29-ounce) can pumpkin puree
- ½ cup brown sugar
- ⅔ cup milk
- 2 tablespoons pumpkin pie spice
- ½ cup sugar
- ¼ cup butter, chilled
- ¾ cup chopped pecans
  Vanilla ice cream

Instructions

1 Preheat oven to 350 F. Grease a 13x9-inch baking dish.

2 Set aside 1 cup of cake mix. In a medium bowl, combine remaining cake mix with melted butter and 1 egg until well blended.

3 Spread mixture in bottom of prepared baking dish.

4 In a large bowl, combine pumpkin, brown sugar, milk, remaining eggs and pumpkin pie spice. Mix well and pour over mixture in baking dish.

5 In a small bowl, combine sugar and reserved cake mix. Use a pastry blender to incorporate chilled butter into mixture until it resembles coarse crumbs.

6 Spoon over pumpkin mixture, and sprinkle chopped pecans over top. Bake 45 to 50 minutes, until top is golden.

7 Serve warm with vanilla ice cream.

Pies & Tarts

Cakes & Cheesecakes

Cookies & Bars

Quick Breads & Muffins

Breads, Rolls & Biscuits

Cobblers, Crisps & Crumbles

Desserts

All photography by Liam Franklin

*Rustic Pear Tart
With Dried Cherries,
p. 16*

CENTENNIAL BOOKS

An Imprint of
Centennial Media, LLC
40 Worth St., 10th Floor
New York, NY 10013, U.S.A.

CENTENNIAL BOOKS is a trademark of Centennial Media, LLC

ISBN 978-1-951274-76-4

Distributed by
Simon & Schuster, Inc.
1230 Avenue of the Americas
New York, NY 10020, U.S.A.

For information about custom editions, special sales and premium and corporate purchases,
please contact Centennial Media at contact@centennialmedia.com.

Manufactured in China

© 2021 by Centennial Media, LLC

10 9 8 7 6 5 4 3 2 1